MW00450641

DINNER IS IN T

Quick and Easy Dinners in Mason Jars

Create a 90 day supply of easily prepared dinners your family will love using food storage ingredients in mason jars or mylar bags for emergencies & convenience on busy days.

By

KATHY CLARK

Also visit us on the web at *DinnerIsInTheJar.com*

Notice:

All rights to *Dinner Is In The Jar* are owned solely by Dinner Is In The Jar, LLC.

Artwork: The artwork added to the 4th Edition is intended to be images of different aspects of self-reliance and independent living.   We hope you enjoy the images and art.

Mention of specific companies, organizations or authorities in this book does not imply endorsement by the author or publisher, nor does mention of specific companies, organizations or authorities imply that they endorse this book, its author, or the publisher.

Internet addresses and telephone numbers given in this book were accurate at the time it went to press.

© 2009, 2010, 2011, 2012 by Dinner Is In The Jar, LLC (4th Edition)

All rights reserved. No part of this publication may be reproduced or transmitted in any form or by any means, electronic or mechanical, including photocopying, recording or any other information storage and retrieval system, without the written permission of the author.

Printed in the United States of America.

ISBN 14-50550924

EAN 13– 9781450550925

For the loves of my life, my beloved and wonderful husband, Colby, and our girls, Sandalyne and Ireland Jade.

Kathy Clark is a devoted wife and full time mother of two wonderful children. She enjoys learning to use food storage and has created these recipes as a way to have a supply of easily prepared meals for busy days while simultaneously using and rotating her food storage. Many friends and family continually asked for her recipes, and so she compiled them into this book to share with all who wanted quick and easy premixed dinners using food storage for use and gifts. She earned a law degree at Loyola Law School of California, and practiced family law in Beverly Hills, California. She has retired to raise her family and now lives in the beautiful Pacific Northwest.

INTRODUCTION

Wouldn't it be nice if your pantry was filled with premixed dinners that you could put together with little effort and have healthy homemade meals that your family would love? Not only would you have a supply of easy dinners, but you could also give them away as gifts. This book is filled with dinner mix recipes that can be easily stored in mason jars or mylar bags.

You can also pre-make as many as you like well in advance. When stored with oxygen absorbers, they last a long time. There is a recipe for each day of the month. If you make 3 of each recipe, you will have a 90 day supply of premixed dinners ready.

Making your own mixes gives you control over the ingredients to suit your taste, dietary concerns, supplies and budget. Moreover, when you prepare the mixes, they cost a faction of the cost of store bought dinner mixes in a box.

The ingredients for these recipes call for food storage items as much as possible. So, if you have food storage, this will allow you to use and rotate your supplies. When meat is called for in a recipe, you can use fresh <u>cooked</u> meat, meat you pressure canned in pint size mason jars, or textured vegetable protein (TVP).

I kept the jar dinners as fresh as possible by vacuum sealing the jars with a household vacuum sealer. I have found that using mylar bags with oxygen absorbers is the best storage solution for powdery recipes such as biscuits, pizza dough mix, etc. This is due to the fact that the seal on vacuum sealed jars containing a lot of powdery substances tends to fail over time. I also recommend checking the seal on your jars every so often. If properly vacuumed sealed, they should not "click" when pushed down in the center. <u>Wide mouth mason jars</u> are the easiest size to use, since they not only are wider but also hold a bit more.

Many of the recipes require the addition of something else such as a can of chopped tomatoes or a pint of chicken. These are called "Add-Ons". They are noted on each recipe.

Because each family is different, we strongly recommend that you try each recipe before producing it in mass. Feel free to change the recipe to suit your tastes and dietary needs.

Many of the recipes taste even better the next day. So, you can prepare a day ahead then re-heat. Most recipes are great garnished with shredded cheese and sour cream.

MENU

ADD-ONS – ITEMS NEEDED IN ADDITION TO MASON JARS

Items	Recipe's Page # (1 can needed per recipe unless noted with "x # cans needed" such as "9 x 2" = page 9, 2 cans needed)	Needed for 90 Day Supply
1 pint cooked chicken[1]	7, 15, 21, 29, 41, 47, 49, 51, 53, 55	30
1 pint cooked ground beef[2]	9 x 2, 13, 17, 19, 27, 31, 33, 35, 43 x 2, 45, 59	39
14 ounce can diced tomatoes[3]	9 x 2, 11, 17 x 2, 25, 27 x 3, 31, 43 x 2, 45 x 2, 49, 53, 57, 59, 61	57
28 oz can crushed tomatoes	37	3
15 oz can tomato sauce	49	3
15 ounce can corn	17	3
4 oz can diced green chiles	53, 59	6
14 oz can green beans	15	3
Small can sliced olives	49, 57, 59	9
15 oz can mixed vegetables	13	3
Grated parmesan cheese	7, 11, 19, 23, 57	5 ½ C + 2 T
1 pound package spaghetti	11	3
4 oz jar Yeast	23, 57	1
Small Jar of Olive Oil	11, 49, 53, 57, 59	1
1 pound Butter	15, 41	1
Ketchup (1/2 c)	43	1

SO, WHERE DO I GET THIS STUFF?

Tip: Review Appendix B in the back of the book for an alphabetical list of ingredients and add-ons needed for all of the recipes. For an up to date list of where to purchase the ingredients, visit us on the web at DinnerIsInTheJar.com and go to the "Ingredients" page.

---

[1] You can pressure can the chicken yourself. You can also substitute turkey which can be obtained over the holidays frequently for $0.90 a pound or less. If you are using fresh chicken, you will need about a pound.

[2] If you can your ground beef, many sources state that you must use super lean ground beef. At about $4 a pound, this is expensive. You may want to use fresh ground beef if you have it on hand or TVP for these recipes instead. One pint of ground beef would be equal to about a pound of fresh, uncooked ground beef. **All recipes assume the meat is already cooked.**

[3] If you have a plentiful harvest of tomatoes in your garden, you can pressure or water bath can the tomatoes for use with these recipes. A pint size jar would equal a can.

KEY TO SHORT CUT SYMBOLS AND ABBREVIATIONS

⏰ This symbol next to a recipe means the recipe is quick and easy to prepare with little work or preparation.

🌙 This symbol next to a recipe means that the recipe requires some overnight preparation, such as soaking the beans.

T = tablespoon
t = teaspoon
c = cup

HOW LARGE ARE THE MEALS?

The meals are designed for the average family of 4. The soups make between 8 and 10 cups. The pizza makes 2 medium size pizzas, and the calzone recipe makes 6 calzones. The biscuit recipes makes 12 biscuits. The meals can be easily halved or doubled.

APPENDIX

Appendix A: (page 67): An alphabetical list of recipes
Appendix B: (page 68): An alphabetical list of ingredients and add-ons for all recipes, plus the amounts needed for a 30, 60 & 90 day supply.

Tip for 90 Day Supply Preparation: Each night, make one of the recipes for dinner. Then, when you put together the ingredients for that night's dinner, have jars lined up on your counter and add the same ingredients into 3 jars (one for each month of the 3 month supply). That way, it takes very little extra time to put it together. Each night do another recipe & 3 jars. After a month, you will have the whole 90 day supply prepared.

USING MYLAR BAGS INSTEAD OF JARS

  Jars can be expensive. So, as an alternative, you can use mylar bags. If you cut the bag in half, and seal up the cut side, you have a quart size bag. It is less expensive than a jar and won't break if it falls. This is also a good option of you plan on mailing dinners as gifts.

  It is best to have an iron specifically designated for this task. Someitmes, the metal from the mylar bag will flake onto the iron. If you are using the same iron that you use for your clothes, the flaked metal from the mylar bag could damage your clothing.

Use a regular mylar bag from the cannery

Fold bag in half along the long side and crease the fold

Cut along crease

Put cut side on a smooth piece of wood or metal

Iron the seam with iron on medium to hot (no steam). It only takes a few seconds or less

Here is what the sealed seam looks like. Try to avoid wrinkles.

Use a funnel to easily fill the bag with ingredients. Remember the oxygen absorber.

Iron the opening to seal it shut

Glue the label to the bag

HOW TO VACUUM SEAL A JAR

Jar Sealer

1. Make sure the rim of the jar is clean and place a lid on top.
2. Put a "Jar Sealer" over the lid. Jar Sealers can be purchased on the internet. Links to purchase a Jar Sealer can be found on DinnerIsInTheJar.com on the Ingredients page.
3. Insert the accesory tube from the vacuum sealer into the Jar Sealer and activiate the accessory tube. In many models of vacuum sealers this is marked as the "Accessory" or "Canister" button. It will then vacuum seal the jar.
4. Once complete, remove tube from Jar Sealer, and then gently remove the Jar Sealer. Your jar will be vacuum sealed.
5. Tip: If the ingredients in the jar are powdery (flour or other powders), then the vacuum will likely not work, as the powders will compromise the jar lids. Mylar bags are better suited for powdery ingredients.
6. Tip: The seal on the lids of the jars should periodicly be checked, since at times the jar lids will break loose.
7. This vacume sealing method, is <u>not</u> the same as pressure canning and should <u>not</u> be used as a method to replace pressure or water bath caninng for food preservation.

ONE SIZE DOES NOT FIT ALL

Because we are all different, what works for one family may not necessarily work for another. We strongly encourage you to try out any recipe before you make it in mass. Often times, one family will enjoy more spice than another, and each recipe should be adjusted to fit your family's tastes, preferences, allergies, and health concerns.

PASTA SOUP ⏰

1 ¾ c macaroni
¾ c. dried chopped mushrooms
3 ½ T. dried minced onion

---- **In a baggie in the jar** ----
¾ c lentils
2 ½ T. Chicken bouillon granules
1 T + 1 t. Italian seasoning
1 T parsley
1 ¾ t. oregano leaves
1/4 t. garlic powder

Add-on: 1 pint cooked chicken cubes
10 ½ c water
½ c Parmesan Cheese[1]

Directions: Remove oxygen absorber. Add contents of **baggie** to water and bring to a boil. Reduce heat and cover. Simmer for 30 minutes. Add the contents of the **jar** (macaroni & mushroom mix), chicken & parmesan cheese and simmer another 15 minutes until lentils and macaroni are tender, stirring occasionally.

---
[1] **Tip:** The Parmesan Cheese is kept out of the jar because it tends to have a higher moisture content and cause ingredients in the jar to cake.

LABELS FOR JARS - FOR PHOTOCOPYING

PASTA SOUP ⏰

Add-on:
1 pint cooked chicken cubes
10 ½ c water
½ c Parmesan cheese

Directions: Remove oxygen absorber. Add contents of **baggie** to water and bring to a boil. Reduce heat and cover. Simmer for 30 minutes. Add the contents of the **jar** (macaroni & mushroom mix), chicken & parmesan cheese and simmer another 15 minutes until lentils and macaroni are tender, stirring occasionally.

PASTA SOUP ⏰

Add-on:
1 pint cooked chicken cubes
10 ½ c water
½ c Parmesan cheese

Directions: Remove oxygen absorber. Add contents of **baggie** to water and bring to a boil. Reduce heat and cover. Simmer for 30 minutes. Add the contents of the **jar** (macaroni & mushroom mix), chicken & parmesan cheese and simmer another 15 minutes until lentils and macaroni are tender, stirring occasionally.

PASTA SOUP ⏰

Add-on:
1 pint cooked chicken cubes
10 ½ c water
½ c Parmesan cheese

Directions: Remove oxygen absorber. Add contents of **baggie** to water and bring to a boil. Reduce heat and cover. Simmer for 30 minutes. Add the contents of the **jar** (macaroni & mushroom mix), chicken & parmesan cheese and simmer another 15 minutes until lentils and macaroni are tender, stirring occasionally.

PASTA SOUP ⏰

Add-on:
1 pint cooked chicken cubes
10 ½ c water
½ c Parmesan cheese

Directions: Remove oxygen absorber. Add contents of **baggie** to water and bring to a boil. Reduce heat and cover. Simmer for 30 minutes. Add the contents of the **jar** (macaroni & mushroom mix), chicken & parmesan cheese and simmer another 15 minutes until lentils and macaroni are tender, stirring occasionally.

CHILI

This is a 1 Quart and 1 Pint dinner

Quart Jar
3 c dried red or kidney beans[1]
¼ t baking soda

Seasoning Baggie
2 T cornstarch

Seasoning Pint
3 T chili powder
½ C + 2 T dried minced onions
1 T dried minced garlic
1 t dried oregano leaves
2 t salt
¼ t cayenne pepper
½ t garlic salt
½ t Italian seasoning
¼ t black pepper
½ c tomato powder
½ c dried chopped bell peppers

Add-on: 2 (14-oz.) cans diced tomatoes
2 pints cooked ground beef, sausage, chicken or TVP
18 c water divided

Directions: Remove oxygen absorber. Soak beans with 8 c. water overnight. Rinse. Place beans in soup pot with 10 c. water. Simmer 1 ½ hours uncovered. Add tomatoes, beef and seasoning **pint**. Simmer 30 minutes more. If it needs to be thicker, mix contents of **baggie** from the quart with some cold water and add to chili. Simmer until thick. Wonderful served on a bed of rice and topped with sour cream and shredded cheese.

---

[1] **Tip:** These can be replaced with 3 15oz cans of red kidney beans or 3 pints of pressure canned red kidney beans. If replaced, skip the soaking & 1 ½ hour cooking.

LABELS FOR JARS - FOR PHOTOCOPYING

CHILI - QUART JAR

Add-ons:
2 (14-oz.) cans diced tomatoes
2 pints cooked ground beef, sausage,
chicken or TVP
18 c water divided

Directions: Remove oxygen absorber. Soak beans with 8 c. water overnight. Rinse. Place beans in soup pot with 10 c. water. Simmer 1 ½ hours uncovered. Add tomatoes, beef and seasoning **pint**. Simmer 30 minutes more. If it needs to be thicker, mix contents of **baggie** from the quart with some cold water and add to chili. Simmer until thick. Wonderful served on a bed of rice and topped with sour cream and shredded cheese.

CHILI – SEASONING PINT

Add-ons:
2 (14-oz.) cans diced tomatoes
2 pints cooked ground beef, sausage, chicken
or TVP
18 c water divided

Directions: Remove oxygen absorber. Soak beans with 8 c. water overnight. Rinse. Place beans in soup pot with 10 c. water. Simmer 1 ½ hours uncovered. Add tomatoes, beef and seasoning **pint**. Simmer 30 minutes more. If it needs to be thicker, mix contents of **baggie** from the quart with some cold water and add to chili. Simmer until thick. Wonderful served on a bed of rice and topped with sour cream and shredded cheese.

CHILI - QUART JAR

Add-ons:
2 (14-oz.) cans diced tomatoes
2 pints cooked ground beef, sausage,
chicken or TVP
18 c water divided

Directions: Remove oxygen absorber. Soak beans with 8 c. water overnight. Rinse. Place beans in soup pot with 10 c. water. Simmer 1 ½ hours uncovered. Add tomatoes, beef and seasoning **pint**. Simmer 30 minutes more. If it needs to be thicker, mix contents of **baggie** from the quart with some cold water and add to chili. Simmer until thick. Wonderful served on a bed of rice and topped with sour cream and shredded cheese.

CHILI – SEASONING PINT

Add-ons:
2 (14-oz.) cans diced tomatoes
2 pints cooked ground beef, sausage, chicken
or TVP
18 c water divided

Directions: Remove oxygen absorber. Soak beans with 8 c. water overnight. Rinse. Place beans in soup pot with 10 c. water. Simmer 1 ½ hours uncovered. Add tomatoes, beef and seasoning **pint**. Simmer 30 minutes more. If it needs to be thicker, mix contents of **baggie** from the quart with some cold water and add to chili. Simmer until thick. Wonderful served on a bed of rice and topped with sour cream and shredded cheese.

SPAGHETTI & MEATBALLS IN MUSHROOM PARMESAN TOMATO SAUCE

Quart 1 - Meatballs
3/4 c sausage TVP
3/4 c beef TVP
1 1/2 T dried minced onions

--- In baggie in jar ---
1/4 c + 2 T vital wheat gluten flour
1 1/2 T egg powder
1 1/2 T seasoned bread crumbs
2 t oregano leaves
2 t Italian seasoning
1 t basil

Quart 2 - Sauce
1/2 c. tomato powder
1/4 c corn starch
1 t garlic powder
1 t oregano leaves
1/4 t black pepper
1 t salt
1/4 t paprika
1/2 c chopped dried mushroom pieces
1 T Italian seasoning
1 t sugar
Pinch cayenne pepper

Add on: 14 oz can diced tomatoes
1/2 c grated parmesan cheese
1 pound package spaghetti
2 T olive oil
5 c water divided

Directions: Remove oxygen absorber.

Quart 1 - Meatballs: Bring 1 1/2 c. water just to a boil, turn heat off & add TVP mix. Cover let sit 10 minutes. Take cover off & simmer until water is boiled off[1], being careful not to burn the TVP. Mix TVP & contents of seasoning baggie then place in a food processor and process until smooth. Form mixture into small teaspoon size balls and place on a greased cookie sheet. Bake at 350 for 20 to 23 minutes.

Quart 2 - Sauce: Mix contents of jar with 3 1/2 cups water using a whisk. Combine the diced tomatoes (with juice) with the parmesan & stir until well blended. Cook over medium heat stirring often until thick.

Cook spaghetti according to package directions and coat with olive oil.

---

[1] The water is boiled off to retain the seasonings from the TVP. If the TVP is drained instead, most of the seasonings are lost.

LABELS FOR JARS - FOR PHOTOCOPYING

SPAGHETTI & MEATBALLS QUART 1 OF 2 - MEATBALLS

Directions for Quart 1: Remove oxygen absorber.

Bring 1 1/2 c. water just to a boil, turn heat off & add TVP mix. Cover let sit 10 minutes. Take cover off & simmer until water is boiled off, being careful not to burn the TVP. Mix TVP & contents of seasoning baggie then place in a food processor and process until smooth. Form mixture into small teaspoon size balls and place on a greased cookie sheet. Bake at 350 for 20 to 23 minutes.

SPAGHETTI & MEATBALLS QUART 2 OF 2 - SAUCE

Add on: 14 oz can diced tomatoes
1/2 c grated parmesan cheese
1 package spaghetti
2 T olive oil

Directions for Quart 2: Remove oxygen absorber.

Mix contents of jar with 3 1/2 cups water using a whisk. Combine the diced tomatoes (with juice) with the parmesan & stir until well blended. Cook over medium heat stirring often until thick.

Cook spaghetti according to package directions. Coat with olive oil.

GROUND BEEF STROGANOFF

This is a 1 Quart and 1 Pint dinner

Quart Jar

2 3/4 c macaroni

-- In a baggie in the jar --

1 c dried mushroom pieces

Seasoning Pint

¼ c. + 2 T sour cream powder
1 c dry milk
1/3 c cornstarch
2 T chicken or beef bouillon
1 T dried minced onion
½ t. dried basil
½ t. dried thyme
¼ t. + 1/8 t. black pepper
1 T. dried parsley
1 ½ t. garlic powder

Add-on: 1 pint cooked ground beef
1 can mixed vegetables (optional)
3 c water divided

Directions: Remove oxygen absorber. Cook and drain macaroni keeping macaroni in colander. Keep hot water. Put mushrooms in hot water & let sit for about 5 minutes until soft, drain. Move seasoning from pint to quart jar (a funnel is helpful for this). Add 2 c. water to quart jar. Put on jar rim & lid & screw tightly closed. Shake and stir jar until sauce is well blended. Add 1 cup more water to jar. Shake. Pour sauce into the pot you cooked the noodles in and whisk out any remaining lumps. Simmer a few minutes until thick, stirring often. Return noodles, mushrooms & meat to pot and mix.

LABELS FOR JARS - FOR PHOTOCOPYING

GROUND BEEF STROGANOFF

Add-ons: 1 pint cooked ground beef
3 c water divided

Directions: Remove oxygen absorber. Cook and drain macaroni keeping macaroni in colander. Keep hot water. Put mushrooms in hot water & let sit for about 5 minutes until soft, drain. Move seasoning from pint to quart jar (a funnel is helpful for this). Add 2 c. water to quart jar. Put on jar rim & lid & screw tightly closed. Shake and stir jar until sauce is well blended. Add 1 cup more water to jar. Shake. Pour sauce into the pot you cooked the noodles in and whisk out any remaining lumps. Simmer a few minutes until thick, stirring often. Return noodles, mushrooms & meat to pot and mix.

GROUND BEEF STROGANOFF

Add-ons: 1 pint cooked ground beef
3 c water divided

Directions: Remove oxygen absorber. Cook and drain macaroni keeping macaroni in colander. Keep hot water. Put mushrooms in hot water & let sit for about 5 minutes until soft, drain. Move seasoning from pint to quart jar (a funnel is helpful for this). Add 2 c. water to quart jar. Put on jar rim & lid & screw tightly closed. Shake and stir jar until sauce is well blended. Add 1 cup more water to jar. Shake. Pour sauce into the pot you cooked the noodles in and whisk out any remaining lumps. Simmer a few minutes until thick, stirring often. Return noodles, mushrooms & meat to pot and mix.

GROUND BEEF STROGANOFF

Add-ons: 1 pint cooked ground beef
3 c water divided

Directions: Remove oxygen absorber. Cook and drain macaroni keeping macaroni in colander. Keep hot water. Put mushrooms in hot water & let sit for about 5 minutes until soft, drain. Move seasoning from pint to quart jar (a funnel is helpful for this). Add 2 c. water to quart jar. Put on jar rim & lid & screw tightly closed. Shake and stir jar until sauce is well blended. Add 1 cup more water to jar. Shake. Pour sauce into the pot you cooked the noodles in and whisk out any remaining lumps. Simmer a few minutes until thick, stirring often. Return noodles, mushrooms & meat to pot and mix.

GROUND BEEF STROGANOFF

Add-ons: 1 pint cooked ground beef
3 c water divided

Directions: Remove oxygen absorber. Cook and drain macaroni keeping macaroni in colander. Keep hot water. Put mushrooms in hot water & let sit for about 5 minutes until soft, drain. Move seasoning from pint to quart jar (a funnel is helpful for this). Add 2 c. water to quart jar. Put on jar rim & lid & screw tightly closed. Shake and stir jar until sauce is well blended. Add 1 cup more water to jar. Shake. Pour sauce into the pot you cooked the noodles in and whisk out any remaining lumps. Simmer a few minutes until thick, stirring often. Return noodles, mushrooms & meat to pot and mix.

CHICKEN & RICE ⏲

2 ½ c white rice
1 T. + 1 t. dried minced onion
1 T. + 1 t. dried bell pepper
2/3 t. parsley
1 t. *each* garlic powder and Italian seasoning
2/3 t. chili powder
1 ½ t. paprika
2/3 t. dried oregano leaves
2/3 t. dried thyme
1 1/2 T. chicken bouillon

Add-on: 1 pint cooked chicken or fried egg
5 c water
3 T. butter
1 can green beans

Directions: Remove oxygen absorber. Mix rice and water in large pot. Top with butter. Cover and cook on medium heat for 15 minutes then adjust to low heat for another 15 minutes. Fluff with a fork. Add chicken, green beans and cover. Let sit for 5 minutes.

LABELS FOR JARS - FOR PHOTOCOPYING

CHICKEN & RICE ⏰

Add-on:

1 pint cooked chicken (or fried egg)

5 c water

3 T. butter

1 can green beans

Directions: Remove oxygen absorber. Mix rice and water in large pot. Top with butter. Cover and cook on medium heat for 15 minutes then adjust to low heat for another 15 minutes. Fluff with a fork. Add chicken/egg, green beans and cover. Let sit for 5 minutes.

CHICKEN & RICE ⏰

Add-on:

1 pint cooked chicken (or fried egg)

5 c water

3 T. butter

1 can green beans

Directions: Remove oxygen absorber. Mix rice and water in large pot. Top with butter. Cover and cook on medium heat for 15 minutes then adjust to low heat for another 15 minutes. Fluff with a fork. Add chicken/egg, green beans and cover. Let sit for 5 minutes.

CHICKEN & RICE ⏰

Add-on:

1 pint cooked chicken (or fried egg)

5 c water

3 T. butter

1 can green beans

Directions: Remove oxygen absorber. Mix rice and water in large pot. Top with butter. Cover and cook on medium heat for 15 minutes then adjust to low heat for another 15 minutes. Fluff with a fork. Add chicken/egg, green beans and cover. Let sit for 5 minutes.

CHICKEN & RICE ⏰

Add-on:

1 pint cooked chicken (or fried egg)

5 c water

3 T. butter

1 can green beans

Directions: Remove oxygen absorber. Mix rice and water in large pot. Top with butter. Cover and cook on medium heat for 15 minutes then adjust to low heat for another 15 minutes. Fluff with a fork. Add chicken/egg, green beans and cover. Let sit for 5 minutes.

Texas Two Step Soup ⏰

½ c brown gravy mix
¼ c chili powder
1 T. + 1 t. dried oregano leaves
2 t. ground cumin
3 t. dried minced onion
1 t. garlic salt
1/8 t. garlic powder
24 tortilla chips coarsely crushed
2 1/3 c macaroni

Add-on: 1 pint cooked ground beef
14 c water
1 – 15 oz. can corn
2 – 16 oz. cans chopped tomatoes

Directions: Remove oxygen absorber. Bring water to boil with soup mix and add-ons. Cover. Simmer 20 minutes. Top individual serving bowls with shredded cheese and sour cream.

Labels for Jars - For Photocopying

Texas Two Step Soup ⏰

Add-on: 1 pint cooked ground beef
14 c water
1 – 15 oz. can corn
2 – 16 oz. cans chopped tomatoes

Directions: Remove oxygen absorber. Bring water to boil with soup mix and add-ons. Cover. Simmer 20 minutes. Top individual serving bowls with shredded cheese and sour cream.

Texas Two Step Soup ⏰

Add-on: 1 pint cooked ground beef
14 c water
1 – 15 oz. can corn
2 – 16 oz. cans chopped tomatoes

Directions: Remove oxygen absorber. Bring water to boil with soup mix and add-ons. Cover. Simmer 20 minutes. Top individual serving bowls with shredded cheese and sour cream.

Texas Two Step Soup ⏰

Add-on: 1 pint cooked ground beef
14 c. water
1 – 15 oz. can corn
2 – 16 oz. cans chopped tomatoes

Directions: Remove oxygen absorber. Bring water to boil with soup mix and add-ons. Cover. Simmer 20 minutes. Top individual serving bowls with shredded cheese and sour cream.

Texas Two Step Soup ⏰

Add-on: 1 pint cooked ground beef
14 c. water
1 – 15 oz. can corn
2 – 16 oz. cans chopped tomatoes

Directions: Remove oxygen absorber. Bring water to boil with soup mix and add-ons. Cover. Simmer 20 minutes. Top individual serving bowls with shredded cheese and sour cream.

SKILLET LASAGNA ⏰

This is a 1 Quart and 1 Pint dinner

Quart Jar	**Seasoning Pint**
3 c macaroni	¼ c. + 2 T. dry milk
	2 T. + 2 t. cornstarch
	2 t. chicken or beef bouillon
	¼ t. dried basil
	¼ t. dried thyme
	1/8 t. black pepper
	1 t. dried parsley
	½ t. garlic powder
	¼ c. dried minced onion
	½ c. tomato powder

Add-on: 1 pint cooked ground beef
1/2 c grated parmesan cheese
Shredded cheese[1] & sour cream
3 c water

Directions: Remove oxygen absorber. Cook and drain noodles. Leave noodles in colander. Move seasoning from pint to quart jar (a funnel is helpful for this). Add grated parmesan cheese and 2 c. water to quart jar. Put on jar rim & lid & screw tightly closed. Shake and stir jar until sauce is well blended. Add 1 cup more water to jar. Shake. Pour sauce into the pot you cooked the noodles in and whisk out any remaining lumps. Simmer a few minutes until thick, stirring often. Return noodles to pot with beef and mix up. Top individual servings with shredded cheese & sour cream.

---

[1] If you are preparing these meals for your emergency supply, you can purchase freeze dried shredded cheese. This is generally quite tasty and will even melt.

LABELS FOR JARS - FOR PHOTOCOPYING

SKILLET LASAGNA QUART JAR ⏰

Add-on: 1 pint cooked ground beef
1/2 c grated parmesan cheese
Shredded cheese & sour cream
3 c water

Directions: Remove oxygen absorber. Cook and drain noodles. Leave noodles in colander. Move seasoning from pint to quart jar (a funnel is helpful for this). Add grated parmesan cheese and 2 c. water to quart jar. Put on jar rim & lid & screw tightly closed. Shake and stir jar until sauce is well blended. Add 1 cup more water to jar. Shake. Pour sauce into the pot you cooked the noodles in and whisk out any remaining lumps. Simmer a few minutes until thick, stirring often. Return noodles to pot with beef and mix up. Top individual servings with shredded cheese & sour cream.

SKILLET LASAGNA SEASONING PINT ⏰

Add-on: 1 pint cooked ground beef
1/2 c grated parmesan cheese
Shredded cheese & sour cream
3 c water

Directions: Remove oxygen absorber. Cook and drain noodles. Leave noodles in colander. Move seasoning from pint to quart jar (a funnel is helpful for this). Add grated parmesan cheese and 2 c. water to quart jar. Put on jar rim & lid & screw tightly closed. Shake and stir jar until sauce is well blended. Add 1 cup more water to jar. Shake. Pour sauce into the pot you cooked the noodles in and whisk out any remaining lumps. Simmer a few minutes until thick, stirring often. Return noodles to pot with beef and mix up. Top individual servings with shredded cheese & sour cream.

CHICKEN NOODLE SOUP ⏱

2 T. dried minced onion
2 T. chicken bouillon
2 T. celery flakes
¼ t. black pepper
1 T. Italian seasoning
1/3 c. dried carrots
1 bay leaf
1 t. garlic powder
½ c. dried mushroom slices
2 c. macaroni
¾ c. rice

Add-ons: 1 pint cooked chicken
12 c. hot water

Directions: Remove oxygen absorber. Mix jar contents with chicken and hot water. Simmer 15-20 minutes. Remove bay leaf.

LABELS FOR JARS - FOR PHOTOCOPYING

CHICKEN NOODLE SOUP ⏰

Add-ons: 1 pint cooked chicken
12 c. hot water

Directions: Remove oxygen absorber. Mix jar contents with chicken and hot water. Simmer 15-20 minutes. Remove bay leaf.

CHICKEN NOODLE SOUP ⏰

Add-ons: 1 pint cooked chicken
12 c. hot water

Directions: Remove oxygen absorber. Mix jar contents with chicken and hot water. Simmer 15-20 minutes. Remove bay leaf.

CHICKEN NOODLE SOUP ⏰

Add-ons: 1 pint cooked chicken
12 c. hot water

Directions: Remove oxygen absorber. Mix jar contents with chicken and hot water. Simmer 15-20 minutes. Remove bay leaf.

CHICKEN NOODLE SOUP ⏰

Add-ons: 1 pint cooked chicken
12 c. hot water

Directions: Remove oxygen absorber. Mix jar contents with chicken and hot water. Simmer 15-20 minutes. Remove bay leaf.

ITALIAN CHEESE & SAUSAGE CALZONE

Makes 6 Calzones
This is a 2 Quart Dinner

In Quart 1	In Quart 2
2 3/4 c. flour + 1 T Italian Seasoning	1/2 c. sausage or pepperoni TVP
2 t. salt + 1/4 c cheddar cheese powder	1/2 c. beef TVP

--- in baggie in jar ---
1/4 c. tomato powder
1 T. cornstarch
1/4 t. garlic powder
1/4 t. oregano leaves
1/8 t. black pepper
1/4 t. salt
pinch paprika
(Mix contents in baggie well)

--- in baggie in jar ---
1 c. dried chopped broccoli

--- in baggie in jar ---
1/4 c. seasoned bread crumbs
1/2 t basil
1/4 t. garlic powder
1/4 t parsley
1 t Italian seasonings
1/4 c. cheddar cheese powder

Add-ons: 2 T grated parmesan cheese, 1 T yeast,[1] 2 T olive oil & 3 c water divided

Directions: Remove oxygen absorber.
Directions for Quart 1: Mix 1 cup warm water with oil. Mix yeast with flour. Mix water & flour mixture. Knead for 5 minutes. Let rise in a greased bowl for 90 minutes. Cut dough into 6 equal parts & roll out each part to a circle on a well floured surface.
Sauce: Whisk contents of baggie, parmesan cheese & 1 cup cold water. Bring to a simmer and simmer on low heat until thick.
Directions for Quart 2: Bring 1 c water just to a boil. Add TVP, cover & let sit 10 minutes. Mix broccoli in with TVP, and simmer until water is gone being careful not to burn TVP. Mix TVP with seasoning baggie.
Assembly: Put tomato sauce on each rolled out dough circle, spreading it evenly to about 1/2 inch of the edges. Put 1/6 of the TVP mixture on half of each dough circle. Fold the dough over and pinch seal the edges well. Bake at 450 for 20 minutes.

---

[1] Yeast will store for quite a long time in the freezer.

LABELS FOR JARS - FOR PHOTOCOPYING

ITALIAN CHEESE & SAUSAGE CALZONE – QUART 1 OF 2

Add-Ons: 1 T yeast, 2 T olive oil
2 T grated parmesan cheese
3 c water divided

Directions: Remove oxygen absorber.
Directions for Quart 1:
Dough: Mix 1 cup warm water with oil. Mix yeast with flour. Mix water & flour mixture. Knead for 5 minutes. Let rise in a greased bowl for 90 minutes. Cut dough into 6 equal parts & roll out each part to a circle on a well floured surface.
Sauce: Whisk contents of baggie, parmesan cheese & 1 cup cold water. Bring to a simmer and simmer on low heat until thick.

ITALIAN CHEESE & SAUSAGE CALZONE – QUART 2 OF 2

Directions: Remove oxygen absorber.
Directions for Quart 2:
Filling: Bring 1 c water just to a boil. Add TVP, cover & let sit 10 minutes. Mix broccoli in with TVP, and simmer until water is gone being careful not to burn TVP. Mix TVP with seasoning baggie.
Assembly: Put tomato sauce on each rolled out dough circle, spreading it evenly to about 1/2 inch of the edges. Put 1/6 of the TVP mixture on half of each dough circle. Fold the dough over and pinch seal the edges well. Bake at 450 for 20 minutes.

Tortilla Soup ⏰

2 c. crushed tortilla chips[1]

----- In a baggie in the jar -----
1 c. long grain rice
2 T. chicken bouillon granules
2 t. lemonade powder with sugar
1 t. dried cilantro
½ t. garlic powder
½ t. ground cumin
½ t. salt
¼ c. dried minced onion

Add-on: 1 can diced tomatoes
10 c. water
Sour cream & shredded cheese

Directions: Remove oxygen absorber. Add water, baggie (rice & seasonings) and tomatoes into soup pot. Bring to a boil and simmer, covered, for 20 minutes. Turn off heat and add tortilla chips. Mix and let sit 5 minutes. Put in individual serving bowls. Top each with a dollop of sour cream and mix it into the soup until soup is creamy. Top with shredded cheese.

---

[1]   This is a great use for the broken pieces of tortilla chips in the bottom of the bag!

LABELS FOR JARS - FOR PHOTOCOPYING

TORTILLA SOUP

Add-on: 1 can diced tomatoes
10 c. water
Sour cream & shredded cheese

Directions: Remove oxygen absorber. Add water, baggie (rice & seasonings) and tomatoes into soup pot. Bring to a boil and simmer, covered, for 20 minutes. Turn off heat and add tortilla chips. Mix and let sit 5 minutes. Put in individual serving bowls. Top each with a dollop of sour cream and mix it into the soup until soup is creamy. Top with shredded cheese.

TORTILLA SOUP

Add-on: 1 can diced tomatoes
10 c. water
Sour cream & shredded cheese

Directions: Remove oxygen absorber. Add water, baggie (rice & seasonings) and tomatoes into soup pot. Bring to a boil and simmer, covered, for 20 minutes. Turn off heat and add tortilla chips. Mix and let sit 5 minutes. Put in individual serving bowls. Top each with a dollop of sour cream and mix it into the soup until soup is creamy. Top with shredded cheese.

TORTILLA SOUP

Add-on: 1 can diced tomatoes
10 c. water
Sour cream & shredded cheese

Directions: Remove oxygen absorber. Add water, baggie (rice & seasonings) and tomatoes into soup pot. Bring to a boil and simmer, covered, for 20 minutes. Turn off heat and add tortilla chips. Mix and let sit 5 minutes. Put in individual serving bowls. Top each with a dollop of sour cream and mix it into the soup until soup is creamy. Top with shredded cheese.

TORTILLA SOUP

Add-on: 1 can diced tomatoes
10 c. water
Sour cream & shredded cheese

Directions: Remove oxygen absorber. Add water, baggie (rice & seasonings) and tomatoes into soup pot. Bring to a boil and simmer, covered, for 20 minutes. Turn off heat and add tortilla chips. Mix and let sit 5 minutes. Put in individual serving bowls. Top each with a dollop of sour cream and mix it into the soup until soup is creamy. Top with shredded cheese.

CHILI TOMATO MAC ⏰

This is a 1 Quart and 1 Pint dinner

Quart Jar	Seasoning Pint
3 c macaroni	½ c. + 2 T. dry milk
	1/3 c. cornstarch
	1 T + 1 t. chicken or beef bouillon
	2 t. dried minced onion
	¼ t. + 1/8 t. dried basil
	¼ t. + 1/8 t. dried thyme
	1/8 t. black pepper
	2 t. dried parsley
	1 t. + 1/8 t. garlic powder
	2 T. chili powder

Add-on: 1 pint cooked ground beef
3 – 15 oz. cans chopped tomatoes
3 c water divided
Shredded cheese & sour cream

Directions: Remove oxygen absorber. Cook and drain noodles leaving noodles in colander. Move seasoning from pint to quart jar (a funnel is helpful for this). Add 2 c. water to quart jar. Put on jar rim & lid & screw tightly closed. Shake and stir jar until sauce is well blended. Add 1 cup more water to jar. Shake. Pour sauce into the pot you cooked the noodles in and whisk out any remaining lumps. Simmer a few minutes until thick, stirring often. Return noodles to pot with beef, drained tomatoes and mix up. Top individual servings with shredded cheese & sour cream.

LABELS FOR JARS - FOR PHOTOCOPYING

CHILI TOMATO MAC – QUART ⏲

Add-on: 1 pint cooked ground beef
3 – 15 oz. cans chopped tomatoes
3 c water divided
Shredded cheese & sour cream

Directions: Remove oxygen absorber. Cook and drain noodles leaving noodles in colander. Move seasoning from pint to quart jar (a funnel is helpful for this). Add 2 c. water to quart jar. Put on jar rim & lid & screw tightly closed. Shake and stir jar until sauce is well blended. Add 1 cup more water to jar. Shake. Pour sauce into the pot you cooked the noodles in and whisk out any remaining lumps. Simmer a few minutes until thick, stirring often. Return noodles to pot with beef, drained tomatoes and mix up. Top individual servings with shredded cheese & sour cream.

CHILI TOMATO MAC ⏲ SEASONING PINT

Add-on: 1 pint cooked ground beef
3 – 15 oz. cans chopped tomatoes
3 c water divided
Shredded cheese & sour cream

Directions: Remove oxygen absorber. Cook and drain noodles leaving noodles in colander. Move seasoning from pint to quart jar (a funnel is helpful for this). Add 2 c. water to quart jar. Put on jar rim & lid & screw tightly closed. Shake and stir jar until sauce is well blended. Add 1 cup more water to jar. Shake. Pour sauce into the pot you cooked the noodles in and whisk out any remaining lumps. Simmer a few minutes until thick, stirring often. Return noodles to pot with beef, drained tomatoes and mix up. Top individual servings with shredded cheese & sour cream.

CHEESY CHICKEN CASSEROLE

This is a 1 Quart and 1 Pint Dinner

Quart	**Seasoning Pint**
2 c. macaroni	3/4 c. chicken gravy powder
1 T. chicken bouillon	3/4 c. milk powder
-- In a baggie in the jar --	1 1/2 T sour cream powder
1 ½ c. long grain white rice	1 1/2 T cheddar cheese powder
2 T. dried bell peppers	1/4 t + 1/8 t garlic salt
2 T. dried celery	1 t Italian seasoning
1 T. dried minced onion	Pinch black pepper & cayenne
1 T. beef or chicken bouillon	1/4 t oregano
	1/4 t garlic powder

Add-on: 1 pint cooked chicken
1 can of mixed vegetables or green beans (optional)
1 c. shredded cheese
9 c. water divided

Directions: Remove oxygen absorber.
Quart - Macaroni: Boil 3 ½ c. water. Add macaroni. Simmer, uncovered, for 13 minutes or until water is almost gone. **Rice:** Empty the baggie with the rice into a second pot and add 2 ½ c. water. Cover and simmer on medium heat for 15 minutes. Adjust heat to low for another 15 minutes.
Pint: Whisk contents of seasoning pint with 3 c water. Simmer a few minutes until thick and powders are cooked, stirring often to assure it does not burn.
Assembly: Mix rice, macaroni, soup mix, chicken and (vegetables if using). Put in greased 9 x 13 casserole. Top with cheese. Bake at 350° for 25-30 minutes.

LABELS FOR JARS - FOR PHOTOCOPYING

CHEESY CHICKEN CASSEROLE
QUART ⏰

Add-ons: 1 pint cooked chicken
1 c. shredded cheese
9 c. water divided
1 can of mixed vegetables or green beans
(optional)

Directions for Quart: Remove oxygen absorber.
Macaroni: Boil 3 ½ c. water. Add macaroni. Simmer, uncovered, for 13 minutes or until water is almost gone.
Rice: Empty the baggie with the rice into a second pot and add 2 ½ c. water. Cover and simmer on medium heat for 15 minutes. Adjust heat to low for another 15 minutes.

CHEESY CHICKEN CASSEROLE
PINT ⏰

Add-ons: 1 pint cooked chicken
1 c. shredded cheese
9 c. water divided
1 can of mixed vegetables or green beans
(optional)

Directions for Pint: Remove oxygen absorber. Whisk contents of seasoning pint with 3 c water. Simmer a few minutes until thick and powders are cooked, stirring often to assure it does not burn.
Assembly: Mix rice, macaroni, soup mix, chicken and (vegetables if using). Put in greased 9 x 13 casserole. Top with cheese. Bake at 350° for 25-30 minutes.

CHEESY CHICKEN CASSEROLE
QUART ⏰

Add-ons: 1 pint cooked chicken
1 c. shredded cheese
9 c. water divided
1 can of mixed vegetables or green beans
(optional)

Directions for Quart: Remove oxygen absorber.
Macaroni: Boil 3 ½ c. water. Add macaroni. Simmer, uncovered, for 13 minutes or until water is almost gone.
Rice: Empty the baggie with the rice into a second pot and add 2 ½ c. water. Cover and simmer on medium heat for 15 minutes. Adjust heat to low for another 15 minutes.

CHEESY CHICKEN CASSEROLE
PINT ⏰

Add-ons: 1 pint cooked chicken
1 c. shredded cheese
9 c. water divided
1 can of mixed vegetables or green beans
(optional)

Directions for Pint: Remove oxygen absorber. Whisk contents of seasoning pint with 3 c water. Simmer a few minutes until thick and powders are cooked, stirring often to assure it does not burn.
Assembly: Mix rice, macaroni, soup mix, chicken and (vegetables if using). Put in greased 9 x 13 casserole. Top with cheese. Bake at 350° for 25-30 minutes.

VEGETABLE & BEEF SOUP ⏰

In the Jar
1/2 c. dried green beans
1 T & 1 t beef bouillon
1 t dried basil
1/2 t dried thyme
1/2 t garlic powder
1/2 c. dried sweet corn
1/2 c. dried peas
1/2 c. dried carrot pieces
2 bay leaves (slip along side of jar)
2 T dried onion pieces
2 T dried bell peppers
2 T dried mushroom pieces
2 T dried celery pieces
1/2 c. rice

Add-Ons: 1 pint cooked ground beef
1 can diced tomatoes
8 c. water
1 t salt
1/4 t black pepper

Directions: Remove oxygen absorber. Bring water to a boil. Turn off heat. Empty & stir jar contents into water. Cover & let sit 5 minutes[1]. Add meat and tomatoes. Return to boil. Lower heat to low & simmer 30 minutes partially covered. Add salt & pepper[2]. Remove 2 bay leaves.

---

[1] Dehydrated vegetables can get tough if put directly into boiling water. Hence, the instructions provide for turning off the heat before adding the vegetables and allowing them to sit in the hot water for 5 minutes to rehydrate. At that point, they can be simmered without making them tough.
[2] The extra salt & pepper are added at the end so that they do not interfere in the rehydration of the vegetables.

LABELS FOR JARS - FOR PHOTOCOPYING

VEGETABLE & BEEF SOUP ⏰

Add-On: 1 pint cooked ground beef
1 can diced tomatoes
8 c. water
1 t salt
¼ t pepper

Directions: Remove oxygen absorber. Bring water to a boil. Turn off heat. Empty & stir jar contents into water. Cover & let sit 5 minutes. Add meat and tomatoes. Return to boil. Lower heat to low & simmer 30 minutes partially covered. Add salt & pepper. Remove 2 bay leaves.

VEGETABLE & BEEF SOUP ⏰

Add-On: 1 pint cooked ground beef
1 can diced tomatoes
8 c. water
1 t salt
¼ t pepper

Directions: Remove oxygen absorber. Bring water to a boil. Turn off heat. Empty & stir jar contents into water. Cover & let sit 5 minutes. Add meat and tomatoes. Return to boil. Lower heat to low & simmer 30 minutes partially covered. Add salt & pepper. Remove 2 bay leaves.

VEGETABLE & BEEF SOUP ⏰

Add-On: 1 pint cooked ground beef
1 can diced tomatoes
8 c. water
1 t salt
¼ t pepper

Directions: Remove oxygen absorber. Bring water to a boil. Turn off heat. Empty & stir jar contents into water. Cover & let sit 5 minutes. Add meat and tomatoes. Return to boil. Lower heat to low & simmer 30 minutes partially covered. Add salt & pepper. Remove 2 bay leaves.

VEGETABLE & BEEF SOUP ⏰

Add-On: 1 pint cooked ground beef
1 can diced tomatoes
8 c. water
1 t salt
¼ t pepper

Directions: Remove oxygen absorber. Bring water to a boil. Turn off heat. Empty & stir jar contents into water. Cover & let sit 5 minutes. Add meat and tomatoes. Return to boil. Lower heat to low & simmer 30 minutes partially covered. Add salt & pepper. Remove 2 bay leaves.

SHEPHERD'S MIX

This is a 2 quart dinner.

QUART 1
1/2 C dried green beans
1/2 C dried sweet corn
1/2 C dried peas
1/2 C dried chopped carrots
2 T dried celery pieces
1 T dried minced onion

QUART 2
2 1/2 c. instant mashed potato flakes
2 T butter powder
2 t buttermilk powder
1/2 t salt
(mix up contents of jar)

Seasoning Packet
1/4 C beef gravy mix
1 T tomato powder
1/2 t oregano leaves
1/2 t marjoram
1/2 t garlic powder
1 t beef bouillon
1/8 t black pepper
(mix up contents of seasoning packet
before putting it in the jar)

Add-Ons: 1 pint cooked beef
7 ½ c. water divided

DIRECTIONS FOR QUART 1: Bring 4 c water to boil. Turn off heat. Add vegetables. Let sit 5 minutes covered. Take off cover & return to a boil. Simmer on low heat about 10 minutes until water is reduced to about 2 cups, and until carrots are tender. Add Seasoning packet & meat. Cook until thick.

DIRECTIONS FOR QUART 2: Bring 3 1/2 c. water to a boil and turn off heat. Add jar contents. Mix briefly & cover. Let sit 5 minutes. Fluff with fork.

ASSEMBLY: Pour meat & vegetables into an 11 x 13 casserole dish. Top with potatoes. Alternatively, you can make a ring out of the potatoes on each plate, with the meat & vegetables placed in the center.

LABELS FOR JARS - FOR PHOTOCOPYING

SHEPHERD'S MIX QUART 1 OF 2

Add-On: 1 pint cooked beef
Directions for Quart 1: Remove oxygen absorber.

Bring 4 c. water to boil. Turn off heat. Add vegetables. Let sit 5 minutes covered. Take off cover & return to a boil. Simmer on low heat about 10 minutes until water is reduced to about 2 cups, and until carrots are tender. Add Seasoning packet & meat. Cook until thick.

SHEPHERD'S MIX QUART 2 OF 2

Directions for Quart 2: Remove oxygen absorber.

Bring 3 1/2 c. water to a boil. Add jar contents. Mix briefly & cover. Let sit 5 minutes. Fluff with fork.

Assembly: Pour meat & vegetables into an 11 x 13 casserole dish. Top with potatoes. In the alternative, you can make a ring out of the potatoes on each plate, with the meat & vegetables placed in the center.

SHEPHERD'S MIX QUART 1 OF 2

Add-On: 1 pint cooked beef
Directions for Quart 1: Remove oxygen absorber.

Bring 4 c. water to boil. Turn off heat. Add vegetables. Let sit 5 minutes covered. Take off cover & return to a boil. Simmer on low heat about 10 minutes until water is reduced to about 2 cups, and until carrots are tender. Add Seasoning packet & meat. Cook until thick.

SHEPHERD'S MIX QUART 2 OF 2

Directions for Quart 2: Remove oxygen absorber.

Bring 3 1/2 c. water to a boil. Add jar contents. Mix briefly & cover. Let sit 5 minutes. Fluff with fork.

Assembly: Pour meat & vegetables into an 11 x 13 casserole dish. Top with potatoes. In the alternative, you can make a ring out of the potatoes on each plate, with the meat & vegetables placed in the center.

PEA & LENTIL SOUP ⏲

¼ c. + 2 T split peas
¼ c. + 2 T lentils
¼ c. + 2 T pearled barley
¼ c. + 2 T macaroni
2 T rice
1 ½ t beef bouillon
1 ½ t garlic powder
2 T celery flakes
2 T parsley flakes
¼ t thyme
1/8 t black pepper
1 T butter powder
1 ½ t dried minced onions
1 T tomato powder
1 bay leaf

Add-On:
8 c. water
1 pound cooked beef

Directions: Remove oxygen absorber. Empty jar into soup pot. Add cooked meat[1] & water. Bring soup to a boil. Cover. Lower heat & simmer for 40 to 50 minutes.

---

[1] This soup is also delicious without the meat.

LABELS FOR JARS - FOR PHOTOCOPYING

PEA & LENTIL SOUP

Add-On: 8 c. water
1 pound cooked beef
Directions: Remove oxygen absorber. Empty jar into soup pot. Add cooked meat & water. Bring soup to a boil. Cover. Lower heat & simmer for 40 to 50 minutes

PEA & LENTIL SOUP

Add-On: 8 c. water
1 pound cooked beef
Directions: Remove oxygen absorber. Empty jar into soup pot. Add cooked meat & water. Bring soup to a boil. Cover. Lower heat & simmer for 40 to 50 minutes

PEA & LENTIL SOUP

Add-On: 8 c. water
1 pound cooked beef
Directions: Remove oxygen absorber. Empty jar into soup pot. Add cooked meat & water. Bring soup to a boil. Cover. Lower heat & simmer for 40 to 50 minutes

PEA & LENTIL SOUP

Add-On: 8 c. water
1 pound cooked beef
Directions: Remove oxygen absorber. Empty jar into soup pot. Add cooked meat & water. Bring soup to a boil. Cover. Lower heat & simmer for 40 to 50 minutes

PEA & LENTIL SOUP

Add-On: 8 c. water
1 pound cooked beef
Directions: Remove oxygen absorber. Empty jar into soup pot. Add cooked meat & water. Bring soup to a boil. Cover. Lower heat & simmer for 40 to 50 minutes

PEA & LENTIL SOUP

Add-On: 8 c. water
1 pound cooked beef
Directions: Remove oxygen absorber. Empty jar into soup pot. Add cooked meat & water. Bring soup to a boil. Cover. Lower heat & simmer for 40 to 50 minutes

REFRIED BEAN SOUP ⏱

2 c. dried refried bean flakes
¼ c. dried minced onions
2 T dried celery flakes
2 T dried diced bell peppers
½ c. dried sweet corn
½ c. rice
1 t cumin
1 t dried minced garlic or garlic powder
1 t beef bouillon
1 pinch cinnamon

Add-Ons: 28 oz can of crushed tomatoes
6 c. water
Shredded cheese, sour cream & crushed tortilla chips

Directions: Remove oxygen absorber. Bring crushed tomatoes & water to a boil. Turn off heat. Add jar contents. Cover & let sit 5 minutes. Return to a simmer & simmer about 15 to 20 minutes until rice is tender. Top individual servings bowls with shredded cheese, sour cream & crushed tortilla chips.

LABELS FOR JARS - FOR PHOTOCOPYING

REFRIED BEAN SOUP ⏰

Add-Ons:
28 oz can of crushed tomatoes
6 c. water
Shredded cheese, sour cream & crushed tortilla chips

Directions: Remove oxygen absorber. Bring crushed tomatoes & water to a boil. Turn off heat. Add jar contents. Cover & let sit 5 minutes. Return to a simmer & simmer about 15 to 20 minutes until rice is tender. Top individual servings bowls with shredded cheese, sour cream & crushed tortilla chips.

REFRIED BEAN SOUP ⏰

Add-Ons:
28 oz can of crushed tomatoes
6 c. water
Shredded cheese, sour cream & crushed tortilla chips

Directions: Remove oxygen absorber. Bring crushed tomatoes & water to a boil. Turn off heat. Add jar contents. Cover & let sit 5 minutes. Return to a simmer & simmer about 15 to 20 minutes until rice is tender. Top individual servings bowls with shredded cheese, sour cream & crushed tortilla chips.

REFRIED BEAN SOUP ⏰

Add-Ons:
28 oz can of crushed tomatoes
6 c. water
Shredded cheese, sour cream & crushed tortilla chips

Directions: Remove oxygen absorber. Bring crushed tomatoes & water to a boil. Turn off heat. Add jar contents. Cover & let sit 5 minutes. Return to a simmer & simmer about 15 to 20 minutes until rice is tender. Top individual servings bowls with shredded cheese, sour cream & crushed tortilla chips.

REFRIED BEAN SOUP ⏰

Add-Ons:
28 oz can of crushed tomatoes
6 c. water
Shredded cheese, sour cream & crushed tortilla chips

Directions: Remove oxygen absorber. Bring crushed tomatoes & water to a boil. Turn off heat. Add jar contents. Cover & let sit 5 minutes. Return to a simmer & simmer about 15 to 20 minutes until rice is tender. Top individual servings bowls with shredded cheese, sour cream & crushed tortilla chips.

GREAT NORTHERN BEAN SOUP

¾ c. dried potato dices
½ c. dried chopped carrots
1 t garlic powder
¾ t thyme
½ t rosemary

----- In a baggie in the jar -----
2 c. great northern beans[1]
¼ t baking soda

Seasoning Packet
1 T lemonade mix with sugar
2 T beef bouillon

Add-Ons: 24 C
water divided

Directions: Remove oxygen absorber. Soak beans & soda[2] in 6 c. water overnight. Drain & rinse. Simmer beans in 12 c water covered for 1 ½ hours on low heat. Drain. Bring 4 ½ c. water to a boil. Turn off heat. Put vegetables into hot water, cover & let sit for 5 minutes. Meanwhile, put beans + 1 ½ C water into food processor and process until smooth. Add beans to vegetables in pot. Return to a simmer & simmer until carrots are soft – about 10 minutes. Add seasoning packet and mix.

---

[1] For convenience, the beans can be replaced with two pints of pressure canned great northern beans. If replaced, skip soaking & 1 ½ hour cooking.
[2] Soaking beans with baking soda helps the digestion of the bean & reduces gas.

LABELS FOR JARS - FOR PHOTOCOPYING

GREAT NORTHERN BEAN SOUP

Directions: Remove oxygen absorber. Soak beans & soda in 6 c. water overnight. Drain & rinse. Simmer beans in 12 c water covered for 1 ½ hours on low heat. Drain. Bring 4 ½ c. water to a boil. Turn off heat. Put vegetables into hot water, cover & let sit for 5 minutes. Meanwhile, put beans + 1 ½ C water into food processor and process until smooth. Add beans to vegetables in pot. Return to a simmer & simmer until carrots are soft – about 10 minutes. Add seasoning packet and mix.

GREAT NORTHERN BEAN SOUP

Directions: Remove oxygen absorber. Soak beans & soda in 6 c. water overnight. Drain & rinse. Simmer beans in 12 c water covered for 1 ½ hours on low heat. Drain. Bring 4 ½ c. water to a boil. Turn off heat. Put vegetables into hot water, cover & let sit for 5 minutes. Meanwhile, put beans + 1 ½ C water into food processor and process until smooth. Add beans to vegetables in pot. Return to a simmer & simmer until carrots are soft – about 10 minutes. Add seasoning packet and mix.

GREAT NORTHERN BEAN SOUP

Directions: Remove oxygen absorber. Soak beans & soda in 6 c. water overnight. Drain & rinse. Simmer beans in 12 c water covered for 1 ½ hours on low heat. Drain. Bring 4 ½ c. water to a boil. Turn off heat. Put vegetables into hot water, cover & let sit for 5 minutes. Meanwhile, put beans + 1 ½ C water into food processor and process until smooth. Add beans to vegetables in pot. Return to a simmer & simmer until carrots are soft – about 10 minutes. Add seasoning packet and mix.

GREAT NORTHERN BEAN SOUP

Directions: Remove oxygen absorber. Soak beans & soda in 6 c. water overnight. Drain & rinse. Simmer beans in 12 c water covered for 1 ½ hours on low heat. Drain. Bring 4 ½ c. water to a boil. Turn off heat. Put vegetables into hot water, cover & let sit for 5 minutes. Meanwhile, put beans + 1 ½ C water into food processor and process until smooth. Add beans to vegetables in pot. Return to a simmer & simmer until carrots are soft – about 10 minutes. Add seasoning packet and mix.

HAWAIIAN HAYSTACK

2 c rice
1 t chicken bouillon

--- In Baggie In Jar ---
1/2 c. chicken gravy powder
1/2 c. milk powder
1 T sour cream powder
1 T cheddar cheese powder
1/4 t garlic salt
1/2 t Italian seasoning
Pinch black pepper & cayenne
1/8 t oregano leaves
1/8 t garlic powder

Add-On: 2 T butter (2 pats)
1 pint cooked chicken
5 c. water divided

Directions: Remove oxygen absorber. Put rice, butter and 3 c water in pot. Cover. Put heat on medium for 15 minutes, then on low for 15 minutes.

Meanwhile, whisk contents of seasoning baggie with 2 c water, and add cooked chicken. Simmer sauce a few minutes until thick and powders are cooked, stirring often to assure it does not burn. To serve, put a bed of rice on plate and top with chicken sauce.

LABELS FOR JARS - FOR PHOTOCOPYING

HAWAIIAN HAYSTACKS ⏰

Add-On: 2 T butter (2 pats)
1 pint cooked chicken
5 c. water divided

Directions Remove oxygen absorber. Rice: Put rice, butter and 3 c water in pot. Cover. Put heat on medium for 15 minutes, then on low for 15 minutes.
Topping: Whisk contents of seasoning baggie with 2 c water, and add cooked chicken. Simmer sauce a few minutes until thick and powders are cooked, stirring often to assure it does not burn.
To serve, put a bed of rice on plate and top with chicken sauce.

HAWAIIAN HAYSTACKS ⏰

Add-On: 2 T butter (2 pats)
1 pint cooked chicken
5 c. water divided

Directions Remove oxygen absorber. Rice: Put rice, butter and 3 c water in pot. Cover. Put heat on medium for 15 minutes, then on low for 15 minutes.
Topping: Whisk contents of seasoning baggie with 2 c water, and add cooked chicken. Simmer sauce a few minutes until thick and powders are cooked, stirring often to assure it does not burn.
To serve, put a bed of rice on plate and top with chicken sauce.

HAWAIIAN HAYSTACKS ⏰

Add-On: 2 T butter (2 pats)
1 pint cooked chicken
5 c. water divided

Directions Remove oxygen absorber. Rice: Put rice, butter and 3 c water in pot. Cover. Put heat on medium for 15 minutes, then on low for 15 minutes.
Topping: Whisk contents of seasoning baggie with 2 c water, and add cooked chicken. Simmer sauce a few minutes until thick and powders are cooked, stirring often to assure it does not burn.
To serve, put a bed of rice on plate and top with chicken sauce.

HAWAIIAN HAYSTACKS ⏰

Add-On: 2 T butter (2 pats)
1 pint cooked chicken
5 c. water divided

Directions Remove oxygen absorber. Rice: Put rice, butter and 3 c water in pot. Cover. Put heat on medium for 15 minutes, then on low for 15 minutes.
Topping: Whisk contents of seasoning baggie with 2 c water, and add cooked chicken. Simmer sauce a few minutes until thick and powders are cooked, stirring often to assure it does not burn.
To serve, put a bed of rice on plate and top with chicken sauce.

HAMBURGER SOUP ⏱

2/3 c. rice
1/3 c. dried minced onion
2/3 c dried minced carrots
2/3 c dried sweet corn

Seasoning Packet
2 T + 1 t beef bouillon
2 t basil
2 t cilantro
2 t garlic powder
2 t chili powder
2 t oregano leaves

Add-On: 2 pints cooked beef
2 cans diced tomatoes (*not* drained)
½ c ketchup
10 c water

Directions: Remove oxygen absorber. Bring water to a boil. Turn off heat. Add rice & vegetables. Let sit 5 minutes. Add beef, tomatoes and ketchup. Return to a simmer. Cover. Simmer about 5 minutes. Add Seasoning Packet[1]. Simmer another 10 - 15 minutes until rice is cooked.

---

[1] The seasonings are added at this point, because if they are added too soon, the salt in the bouillon may affect the rehydration of the vegetables.

Labels for Jars - For Photocopying

HAMBURGER SOUP ⏰

Add-On: 2 pints cooked beef
2 cans diced tomatoes (*not* drained)
½ c ketchup
10 c water

Directions: Remove oxygen absorber. Bring water to a boil. Turn off heat. Add rice & vegetables. Let sit 5 minutes. Add beef, tomatoes and ketchup. Return to a simmer. Cover. Simmer about 5 minutes. Add Seasoning Packet. Simmer another 10 - 15 minutes until rice is cooked.

HAMBURGER SOUP ⏰

Add-On: 2 pints cooked beef
2 cans diced tomatoes (*not* drained)
½ c ketchup
10 c water

Directions: Remove oxygen absorber. Bring water to a boil. Turn off heat. Add rice & vegetables. Let sit 5 minutes. Add beef, tomatoes and ketchup. Return to a simmer. Cover. Simmer about 5 minutes. Add Seasoning Packet. Simmer another 10 - 15 minutes until rice is cooked.

HAMBURGER SOUP ⏰

Add-On: 2 pints cooked beef
2 cans diced tomatoes (*not* drained)
½ c ketchup
10 c water

Directions: Remove oxygen absorber. Bring water to a boil. Turn off heat. Add rice & vegetables. Let sit 5 minutes. Add beef, tomatoes and ketchup. Return to a simmer. Cover. Simmer about 5 minutes. Add Seasoning Packet. Simmer another 10 - 15 minutes until rice is cooked.

HAMBURGER SOUP ⏰

Add-On: 2 pints cooked beef
2 cans diced tomatoes (*not* drained)
½ c ketchup
10 c water

Directions: Remove oxygen absorber. Bring water to a boil. Turn off heat. Add rice & vegetables. Let sit 5 minutes. Add beef, tomatoes and ketchup. Return to a simmer. Cover. Simmer about 5 minutes. Add Seasoning Packet. Simmer another 10 - 15 minutes until rice is cooked.

TACO SOUP

In the Jar
1/2 c. dried sweet corn
2 T dried chopped bell peppers
2 T dried minced onions
1/4 c. ranch dressing mix
2 T chili powder
1 t garlic powder
1/4 t onion powder
1/4 t oregano leaves
1/2 t paprika
2 t cumin
1 t seasoning salt
1/8 t black pepper
Pinch cayenne pepper

-- In a baggie in the jar --
1/2 c. pinto beans (remove rocks!)
1/2 c. great northern beans
1/4 t baking soda

Add-Ons: 1 pint cooked beef
2 cans diced tomatoes
16 c. water divided
Shredded cheese
Sour cream
Crushed tortilla chips

Directions: Remove oxygen absorber. Soak beans & soda in 4 c. water overnight. Drain & rinse. Simmer beans in 6 c of water covered for 2 hours on low heat. (This can be done in advance) Drain. Return beans to pot, add 6 cups water, tomatoes (undrained) & beef. Bring to a boil. Turn heat off. Put remainder of jar contents into pot. Cover & let sit 5 minutes. Return to a simmer. Cover & simmer about 10 to 15 minutes. Top individual bowls with shredded cheese, sour cream and crushed tortilla chips.

LABELS FOR JARS - FOR PHOTOCOPYING

TACO SOUP 🌙

Add-Ons: 1 pint cooked beef
2 cans diced tomatoes
16 c. water divided
Shredded cheese, sour cream & crushed tortilla chips

Directions: Remove oxygen absorber. Soak beans & soda in 4 c. water overnight. Drain & rinse. Simmer beans in 6 c of water covered for 2 hours on low heat. (This can be done in advance) Drain. Return beans to pot, add 6 cups water, tomatoes (<u>undrained</u>) & beef. Bring to a boil. Turn heat off. Put remainder of jar contents into pot. Cover & let sit 5 minutes. Return to a simmer. Cover & simmer about 10 to 15 minutes. Top individual bowls with shredded cheese, sour cream and crushed tortilla chips.

TACO SOUP 🌙

Add-Ons: 1 pint cooked beef
2 cans diced tomatoes
16 c. water divided
Shredded cheese, sour cream & crushed tortilla chips

Directions: Remove oxygen absorber. Soak beans & soda in 4 c. water overnight. Drain & rinse. Simmer beans in 6 c of water covered for 2 hours on low heat. (This can be done in advance) Drain. Return beans to pot, add 6 cups water, tomatoes (<u>undrained</u>) & beef. Bring to a boil. Turn heat off. Put remainder of jar contents into pot. Cover & let sit 5 minutes. Return to a simmer. Cover & simmer about 10 to 15 minutes. Top individual bowls with shredded cheese, sour cream and crushed tortilla chips.

TACO SOUP 🌙

Add-Ons: 1 pint cooked beef
2 cans diced tomatoes
16 c. water divided
Shredded cheese, sour cream & crushed tortilla chips

Directions: Remove oxygen absorber. Soak beans & soda in 4 c. water overnight. Drain & rinse. Simmer beans in 6 c of water covered for 2 hours on low heat. (This can be done in advance) Drain. Return beans to pot, add 6 cups water, tomatoes (<u>undrained</u>) & beef. Bring to a boil. Turn heat off. Put remainder of jar contents into pot. Cover & let sit 5 minutes. Return to a simmer. Cover & simmer about 10 to 15 minutes. Top individual bowls with shredded cheese, sour cream and crushed tortilla chips.

TACO SOUP 🌙

Add-Ons: 1 pint cooked beef
2 cans diced tomatoes
16 c. water divided
Shredded cheese, sour cream & crushed tortilla chips

Directions: Remove oxygen absorber. Soak beans & soda in 4 c. water overnight. Drain & rinse. Simmer beans in 6 c of water covered for 2 hours on low heat. (This can be done in advance) Drain. Return beans to pot, add 6 cups water, tomatoes (<u>undrained</u>) & beef. Bring to a boil. Turn heat off. Put remainder of jar contents into pot. Cover & let sit 5 minutes. Return to a simmer. Cover & simmer about 10 to 15 minutes. Top individual bowls with shredded cheese, sour cream and crushed tortilla chips.

CREAMY CHICKEN NOODLE SOUP ⏰

This is a 2 Quart Dinner

Quart 1	**Quart 2**
1 ¼ c macaroni	1 c chicken gravy powder
½ c rice	1 c milk powder
½ c dried chopped carrots	2 T sour cream powder
3 T dried minced onions	2 T cheddar cheese powder
1 T chicken bouillon	1/2 t garlic salt
1 T + 2 t Italian Seasonings	
3/4 t garlic powder	
¼ t black pepper	
1/8 t cayenne pepper	
1/4 t oregano leaves	

Add-On: 1 pint cooked chicken & 11 C water divided

Directions: Remove oxygen absorber.

Quart #1: Bring 7 cups of water to a boil. Turn heat off. Add jar contents, cover & let rest for 5 minutes. Return to a boil & simmer 15 minutes until pasta is cooked & rice is tender.

Quart #2: Whisk contents of quart #2 with 4 c water. Add to soup pot with cooked chicken, stirring until mixed. Simmer a few minutes until thick and powders are cooked. If too thin, add ¼ c flour mixed with a bit of cold water and cook till thickened.

LABELS FOR JARS - FOR PHOTOCOPYING

CREAMY CHICKEN NOODLE SOUP
QUART 1 OF 2 ⏰

Directions: Remove oxygen absorber.
Quart #1: Bring 7 cups of water to a boil. Turn heat off. Add jar contents, cover & let rest for 5 minutes. Return to a boil & simmer 15 minutes until pasta is cooked & rice is tender.
   Once done, follow directions for Quart 2

CREAMY CHICKEN NOODLE SOUP
QUART 2 OF 2 ⏰
Add-On: 1 pint cooked chicken

Directions: Remove oxygen absorber.
Quart #2: Whisk contents of quart #2 with 4 c water. Add to soup pot with cooked chicken, stirring until mixed. Simmer a few minutes until thick and powders are cooked.

CREAMY CHICKEN NOODLE SOUP
QUART 1 OF 2 ⏰

Directions: Remove oxygen absorber.
Quart #1: Bring 7 cups of water to a boil. Turn heat off. Add jar contents, cover & let rest for 5 minutes. Return to a boil & simmer 15 minutes until pasta is cooked & rice is tender.
   Once done, follow directions for Quart 2

CREAMY CHICKEN NOODLE SOUP
QUART 2 OF 2 ⏰
Add-On: 1 pint cooked chicken

Directions: Remove oxygen absorber.
Quart #2: Whisk contents of quart #2 with 4 c water. Add to soup pot with cooked chicken, stirring until mixed. Simmer a few minutes until thick and powders are cooked.

RED CHICKEN ENCHILADA

In the Jar
3 c. flour
1 tsp salt

In Baggie in Jar
1/4 c. cornstarch (blended with other
ingredients in bag)
1/2 t each of oregano leaves, cumin,
garlic powder & salt
1 1/2 t beef bouillon

Add-On: 1 pint cooked chicken
1/3 c. olive oil
15 oz can tomato sauce
1 can diced tomatoes
1 small can sliced olives
3 c. water divided & Shredded
cheese

Making Tortillas: Mix flour mixture with olive oil and 1 cup water. Let dough rest a few minutes. Divide it into 8 balls. Lightly flour your working surface & rolling pin. Roll out each ball to about an 8 inch circle. Place on hot griddle, cook and turn over to other side.

Making Enchilada Sauce: Mix seasoning packet well with 1 cup cold water in pot. Add another cup water & tomato sauce. Cook until thickened.

Assembly: Mix chicken, drained diced tomatoes, & drained olives in a bowl. Mix about ½ c enchilada sauce with chicken. Put about a 1/2 cup of enchilada sauce in bottom of 9 x 13 casserole dish. Dip each tortilla in the enchilada sauce. Fill with chicken mixture and cheese. Roll and place seam side down in casserole dish. Top with any remaining sauce, chicken & cheese. Bake 350 for 30 minutes.

LABELS FOR JARS - FOR PHOTOCOPYING

RED CHICKEN ENCHILADA

Add-On: 1 pint cooked chicken
1/3 c. olive oil
15 oz can tomato sauce
1 can diced tomatoes
1 small can sliced olives
3 c. water divided
Shredded cheese

First, remove oxygen absorber.
Making Tortillas: Mix flour mixture with olive oil and 1 cup water. Let dough rest a few minutes. Divide it into 8 balls. Lightly flour your working surface & rolling pin. Roll out each ball to about an 8 inch circle. Place on hot griddle, cook and turn over to other side.
Making Enchilada Sauce: Mix seasoning packet well with 1 cup cold water in pot. Add another cup water & tomato sauce. Cook until thickened.
Assembly: Mix chicken, drained diced tomatoes, & drained olives in a bowl. Mix about ½ c enchilada sauce with chicken. Put about a 1/2 cup of enchilada sauce in bottom of 9 x 13 casserole dish. Dip each tortilla in the enchilada sauce. Fill with chicken mixture and cheese. Roll and place seam side down in casserole dish. Top with any remaining sauce, chicken & cheese. Bake 350 for 30 minutes.

RED CHICKEN ENCHILADA

Add-On: 1 pint cooked chicken
1/3 c. olive oil
15 oz can tomato sauce
1 can diced tomatoes
1 small can sliced olives
3 c. water divided
Shredded cheese

First, remove oxygen absorber.
Making Tortillas: Mix flour mixture with olive oil and 1 cup water. Let dough rest a few minutes. Divide it into 8 balls. Lightly flour your working surface & rolling pin. Roll out each ball to about an 8 inch circle. Place on hot griddle, cook and turn over to other side.
Making Enchilada Sauce: Mix seasoning packet well with 1 cup cold water in pot. Add another cup water & tomato sauce. Cook until thickened.
Assembly: Mix chicken, drained diced tomatoes, & drained olives in a bowl. Mix about ½ c enchilada sauce with chicken. Put about a 1/2 cup of enchilada sauce in bottom of 9 x 13 casserole dish. Dip each tortilla in the enchilada sauce. Fill with chicken mixture and cheese. Roll and place seam side down in casserole dish. Top with any remaining sauce, chicken & cheese. Bake 350 for 30 minutes

CHICKEN POT PIE
This is a 2 jar dinner.

PINT	QUART
1/2 c. dried potato dices	1 1/2 c flour
1/2 c. dried sweet corn	1/2 t salt
1/2 c. dried peas	1 t baking powder
1/4 c. dried chopped carrots	1/2 T white sugar
1 T dried minced onion	1/2 c shortening powder
Add-On: 1 pint cooked chicken	**--- In Baggie in jar ---**
6 ¼ c. water divided	1/2 c chicken gravy mix
	1/2 c. powdered milk
	1 T sour cream powder
	1 T cheddar cheese powder
	1/4 t garlic salt
	1/2 t Italian seasoning
	Pinch black pepper & cayenne
	1/8 t oregano leaves & garlic powder

First, remove oxygen absorber.

DIRECTIONS FOR FILLING: Bring 4 c water to boil. Turn off heat. Add contents of **pint** (vegetables). Let sit 5 minutes covered. Take off cover & return to a boil. Simmer on low heat about 10-15 minutes until carrots are tender. Drain. Take **seasoning baggie** from **quart** & whisk with 2 c water. Simmer, stirring often, for a few minutes until thick and powders are cooked. Mix in vegetables and chicken.

DIRECTIONS FOR CRUST: Mix flour from **quart** in bowl until well blended. Take 1/4 cup of flour mixture out & place in another small bowl. Add 1/4 c water to the 1/4 c flour mixture and mix well using a whisk until all lumps are gone. Then add water mixture to rest of flour and mix until it forms a nice ball of dough. You may want to add more water depending on the texture of the dough ball. Wrap it in plastic wrap & put in fridge for 30 minutes or longer. Take out of fridge. Cut slightly half off (one half is slightly larger than the other half). Lightly dust your working surface & rolling pin. Roll out larger half of dough and place in the bottom of the well greased pie tin. It may seem like it will not roll out big enough, but keep rolling, it will. Fill with chicken mixture. Roll out second half of dough & top. Cut slits in it to vent. Bake at 350 for 40 to 50 minutes.

LABELS FOR JARS - FOR PHOTOCOPYING

CHICKEN POT PIE - PINT

Add-ons: 1 pint cooked chicken
6 ¼ c. water divided

First, remove oxygen absorber.
DIRECTIONS FOR FILLING: Bring 4 c water to boil. Turn off heat. Add contents of **pint** (vegetables). Let sit 5 minutes covered. Take off cover & return to a boil. Simmer on low heat about 10-15 minutes until carrots are tender. Drain. Take **seasoning baggie** from **quart** & whisk with 2 c water. Simmer, stirring often, for a few minutes until thick and powders are cooked. Mix in vegetables and chicken.

CHICKEN POT PIE - QUART

First, remove oxygen absorber.
DIRECTIONS FOR CRUST: Mix flour from **quart** in bowl until well blended. Take 1/4 cup of flour mixture out & place in another small bowl. Add 1/4 c water to the 1/4 c flour mixture and mix well using a whisk until all lumps are gone. Then add water mixture to rest of flour and mix until it forms a nice ball of dough. You may want to add more water depending on the texture of the dough ball. Wrap it in plastic wrap & put in fridge for 30 minutes or longer. Take out of fridge. Cut slightly half off (one half is slightly larger than the other half). Lightly dust your working surface & rolling pin. Roll out larger half of dough and place in the bottom of the well greased pie tin. It may seem like it will not roll out big enough, but keep rolling, it will. Fill with chicken mixture. Roll out second half of dough & top. Cut slits in it to vent. Bake at 350 for 40 to 50 minutes.

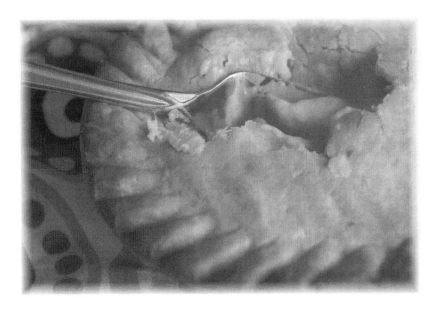

WHITE CHICKEN ENCHILADA

In the Jar
3 c. flour
1 tsp salt (mix with flour before
putting
in jar)

In a Baggie in the Jar
1/4 c. + 2 T flour
1/4 c. sour cream powder

1 T + 1 t dried minced onions
1 t garlic powder
1/4 t black pepper
1 t chicken bouillon

Add-On: 1 pint cooked chicken
1/3 c. olive oil
4 oz can of diced green chiles
1 can diced tomatoes
4 c. water divided
Shredded cheese

First, remove oxygen absorber.

Making Tortillas: Mix flour mixture with olive oil and 1 cup water. Let dough rest a few minutes. Divide it into 8 balls. Lightly flour your working surface & rolling pin. Roll out each ball to about an 8 inch circle. Place on hot griddle, cook and turn over to other side.

Making Enchilada Sauce: Mix seasoning packet well with 1 cup cold water in pot, using a whisk. Add another 2 cups water & green chiles. Cook until bubbly & thickened.

Assembly: Mix chicken with drained diced tomatoes in a bowl. Mix about ½ c enchilada sauce with chicken. Put about a 1/2 cup of enchilada sauce in bottom of 9 x 13 casserole dish. Dip each tortilla in the enchilada sauce. Fill with chicken mixture and cheese. Roll and place seam side down in casserole dish. Top with any remaining sauce, chicken & cheese. Bake 350 for 30 minutes.

LABELS FOR JARS - FOR PHOTOCOPYING

WHITE CHICKEN ENCHILADA

Add-On: 1 pint cooked chicken
1/3 c. olive oil
4 oz can of diced green chiles
1 can diced tomatoes
4 c. water divided
Shredded cheese

Making Tortillas: Mix flour mixture with olive oil and 1 cup water. Let dough rest a few minutes. Divide it into 8 balls. Lightly flour your working surface & rolling pin. Roll out each ball to about an 8 inch circle. Place on hot griddle, cook and turn over to other side.

Making Enchilada Sauce: Mix seasoning packet well with 1 cup cold water in pot, using a whisk. Add another 2 cups water & green chiles. Cook until bubbly & thickened.

Assembly: Mix chicken with drained diced tomatoes in a bowl. Mix about ½ c enchilada sauce with chicken. Put about a 1/2 cup of enchilada sauce in bottom of 9 x 13 casserole dish. Dip each tortilla in the enchilada sauce. Fill with chicken mixture and cheese. Roll and place seam side down in casserole dish. Top with any remaining sauce, chicken & cheese. Bake 350 for 30 minutes.

WHITE CHICKEN ENCHILADA

Add-On: 1 pint cooked chicken
1/3 c. olive oil
4 oz can of diced green chiles
1 can diced tomatoes
4 c. water divided
Shredded cheese

Making Tortillas: Mix flour mixture with olive oil and 1 cup water. Let dough rest a few minutes. Divide it into 8 balls. Lightly flour your working surface & rolling pin. Roll out each ball to about an 8 inch circle. Place on hot griddle, cook and turn over to other side.

Making Enchilada Sauce: Mix seasoning packet well with 1 cup cold water in pot, using a whisk. Add another 2 cups water & green chiles. Cook until bubbly & thickened.

Assembly: Mix chicken with drained diced tomatoes in a bowl. Mix about ½ c enchilada sauce with chicken. Put about a 1/2 cup of enchilada sauce in bottom of 9 x 13 casserole dish. Dip each tortilla in the enchilada sauce. Fill with chicken mixture and cheese. Roll and place seam side down in casserole dish. Top with any remaining sauce, chicken & cheese. Bake 350 for 30 minutes.

BISCUITS & CHICKEN GRAVY

This is a 2 Quart dinner

Quart 1	**Quart 2**
2 c. + 2 T flour	1 c. dried mushroom pieces
5 T dehydrated shortening	1 c. dried broccoli pieces
3 T powdered milk	1 T dried minced onions
2 T dehydrated egg	
1 scant T baking powder	**In a separate baggie in jar**
1 t salt	1/2 c + 1 T chicken gravy powder
1/2 t cream of tartar	2 T sour cream powder
1/4 t baking soda	2 T cheddar cheese powder
	1 t Italian seasoning
	1/4 t garlic powder
	1/4 t onion powder
	1/8 t black pepper
	3 pinches of cayenne

Add-On: 1 pint cooked chicken
8 c. water divided

Directions: First remove oxygen absorber.

Quart 1 Biscuits: Mix flour mixture with 1 cup water. Stir vigorously until well blended. Drop by about 1/4 cup amounts onto a greased baking sheet. You should get about 12 biscuits. Bake at 400 for 10 to 12 minutes.

Quart 2 Gravy: Bring 4 c water to a boil. Turn heat off. Add vegetables, cover & let sit 5 minutes. Return to a low simmer for a few minutes until tender. Drain. Mix with chicken.   In separate pot, mix contents of baggie with 3 c water using a whisk until smooth. Bring to a simmer and turn heat down to low until thick. Add vegetables & chicken.

Assembly: Cut biscuits in half and top with chicken gravy.

Labels for Jars - For Photocopying

Biscuits & Chicken Gravy Quart 1 of 2 - Biscuits

Directions: First remove oxygen absorber.
Quart 1 Biscuits: Mix flour mixture with 1 cup water. Stir vigorously until well blended. Drop by about 1/4 cup amounts onto a greased baking sheet. You should get about 12 biscuits. Bake at 400 for 10 to 12 minutes.

Biscuits & Chicken Gravy Quart 2 of 2 - Gravy

Add-On: 1 pint cooked chicken
8 c. water divided

Directions: First remove any oxygen absorber in jars.
Quart 2 Gravy: Bring 4 c water to a boil. Turn heat off. Add vegetables, cover & let sit 5 minutes. Return to a low simmer for a few minutes until tender. Drain. Mix with chicken. In separate pot, mix contents of baggie with 3 c water using a whisk until smooth. Bring to a simmer and turn heat down to low until thick. Add vegetables & chicken.
Assembly: Cut biscuits in half and top with chicken gravy.

PIZZA IN A JAR

Makes 2 12" pizzas

In Jar

2 3/4 c. flour + 1 T Italian Seasoning

2 t. salt + 1/4 c cheddar cheese powder

--- in baggie in jar ---	Add-On: 1 T. yeast
1/2 c. tomato powder	2 T olive oil
2 T. cornstarch	1/4 c. grated parmesan cheese
1/2 t. garlic powder	1 can diced tomatoes
1/2 t. oregano leaves	1 small can sliced olives (optional)
1/4 t. black pepper	3 c. water divided
1/2 t. salt	Shredded cheese
1/8 t. paprika	Any other topping you please
(Mix contents in baggie well)	

Crust: Mix 1 cup warm water with oil. Mix yeast with flour. Mix water & flour mixture. Knead for 5 minutes. Let rise in a greased bowl for 90 minutes. Roll out each half of the dough into a 12" circle on a well floured surface. **For thick crust**, let rise another 45-50 minutes, then top with sauce & toppings. **For thin crust**, no need for second rising, just roll out and top with sauce & toppings.

Sauce: Whisk contents of baggie, grated parmesan cheese & 2 cups cold water. Bring to a simmer and simmer on low heat until thick.

Bake at 425 for 20 to 25 minutes.

LABELS FOR JARS - FOR PHOTOCOPYING

PIZZA

Add-Ons: 1 T yeast
2 T olive oil
1/4 C grated parmesan cheese
1 can diced tomatoes
1 small can sliced olives
3 c. water divided
Shredded cheese
Any other toppings you please

Directions: Remove oxygen absorber.
Crust: Mix 1 cup warm water with oil. Mix yeast with flour. Mix water & flour mixture. Knead for 5 minutes. Let rise in a greased bowl for 90 minutes. Roll out each half of the dough into a 12" circle on a well floured surface. For thick crust, let rise another 45-50 minutes, then top with sauce & toppings. For thin crust, no need for second rising, just roll out and top with sauce & toppings.
Sauce: Whisk contents of baggie, grated parmesan cheese & 2 cups cold water. Bring to a simmer and simmer on low heat until thick.
Bake at 425 for 20 to 25 minutes. Use extra sauce to dip bread sticks in.

PIZZA

Add-Ons: 1 T yeast
2 T olive oil
1/4 C grated parmesan cheese
1 can diced tomatoes
1 small can sliced olives
3 c. water divided
Shredded cheese
Any other toppings you please

Directions: Remove oxygen absorber.
Crust: Mix 1 cup warm water with oil. Mix yeast with flour. Mix water & flour mixture. Knead for 5 minutes. Let rise in a greased bowl for 90 minutes. Roll out each half of the dough into a 12" circle on a well floured surface. For thick crust, let rise another 45-50 minutes, then top with sauce & toppings. For thin crust, no need for second rising, just roll out and top with sauce & toppings.
Sauce: Whisk contents of baggie, grated parmesan cheese & 2 cups cold water. Bring to a simmer and simmer on low heat until thick.
Bake at 425 for 20 to 25 minutes. Use extra sauce to dip bread sticks in.

MEXICAN PIZZA
This is a 2 Quart dinner

Quart 1	**Quart 2**
3 c. flour	2 c. refried bean chips
1 tsp salt (mix with flour in jar)	1/2 c. dried chopped bell peppers
	1/4 c taco TVP
	1/2 c. dried minced onions
	3 T taco seasoning
	1 t. garlic powder

Add-On: 1 pint cooked ground beef
1/3 c. olive oil
4 oz can of diced green chiles
1 can diced tomatoes
1 can small diced olives
4 c. water divided
Shredded cheese

First, remove oxygen absorber.

Making Tortillas: Mix flour mixture with olive oil and 1 cup water. Let dough rest a few minutes. Divide it into 8 balls. Lightly flour your working surface & rolling pin. Roll out each ball to about an 8 inch circle. Place on hot griddle, cook and turn over to other side. Cook till crisp.

Making filling: Bring 3 c. water to boil. Add contents of Quart #2, green chiles, and cooked ground beef. Stir briefly, cover & turn heat off. Let sit 5 minutes.

Assembly: Place 4 tortillas out on 2 cookie sheets. Top each with 1/4 of filling and then top each with a second tortilla. Sprinkle top tortilla with cheese, tomatoes, and olives. Bake 400 for 8 to 10 minutes.

LABELS FOR JARS - FOR PHOTOCOPYING

MEXICAN PIZZA
QUART 1 OF 2

Add-On: 1/3 c. olive oil
4 c. water divided

First, remove oxygen absorber.
Making Tortillas: Mix flour mixture with olive oil and 1 cup water. Let dough rest a few minutes. Divide it into 8 balls. Lightly flour your working surface & rolling pin. Roll out each ball to about an 8 inch circle. Place on hot griddle, cook and turn over to other side. Cook till crisp.

MEXICAN PIZZA
QUART 2 OF 2

Add-On: 1 pint cooked ground beef
4 oz can of diced green chiles
1 can diced tomatoes
1 can small diced olives
Shredded cheese

First, remove oxygen absorber.
Making filling: Bring 3 c. water to boil. Add contents of Quart #2, green chiles, and cooked ground beef. Stir briefly, cover & turn heat off. Let sit 5 minutes.
Assembly: Place 4 tortillas out on 2 cookie sheets. Top each with 1/4 of filling and then top each with a second tortilla. Sprinkle top tortilla with cheese, tomatoes, and olives. Bake 400 for 8 to 10 minutes.

MEXICAN PIZZA
QUART 1 OF 2

Add-On: 1/3 c. olive oil
4 c. water divided

First, remove oxygen absorber.
Making Tortillas: Mix flour mixture with olive oil and 1 cup water. Let dough rest a few minutes. Divide it into 8 balls. Lightly flour your working surface & rolling pin. Roll out each ball to about an 8 inch circle. Place on hot griddle, cook and turn over to other side. Cook till crisp.

MEXICAN PIZZA
QUART 2 OF 2

Add-On: 1 pint cooked ground beef
4 oz can of diced green chiles
1 can diced tomatoes
1 can small diced olives
Shredded cheese

First, remove oxygen absorber.
Making filling: Bring 3 c. water to boil. Add contents of Quart #2, green chiles, and cooked ground beef. Stir briefly, cover & turn heat off. Let sit 5 minutes.
Assembly: Place 4 tortillas out on 2 cookie sheets. Top each with 1/4 of filling and then top each with a second tortilla. Sprinkle top tortilla with cheese, tomatoes, and olives. Bake 400 for 8 to 10 minutes.

BLACK BEANS & RICE

This is a 1 Quart and 1 Pint Dinner

Quart	**Pint**
1 1/2 c. dried refried bean chips	2 c. rice
1 c. dried sweet corn	1 t. chicken or beef bouillon
2 T dried minced onions	
3 T taco seasonings	

--- In baggie in jar ---
2/3 c. black beans[1]
1/4 t. baking soda

Add Ons: 1 can diced tomatoes
15 c. water divided

Directions: Remove oxygen absorber.
Quart: Soak beans & soda in 4 c. water overnight. Rinse. Simmer beans in 6 c water covered for 1 1/2 hours on low heat. (This can be done in advance) Drain. Return beans to pot, add diced tomatoes undrained, and 2 c. water. Bring to a boil. Turn heat off. Add the rest of the contents of the Quart. Let sit 5 minutes covered. Return to boil and simmer on low heat for 15 minutes.
Pint Rice: Empty the pint into a second pot and add 3 c. water. Cover and simmer on medium heat for 15 minutes. Adjust heat to low for another 15 minutes.
Assembly: Serve beans over a bed of rice.

---

[1] For convenience, this can be replaced with a pint of pressure canned black beans or one 15 oz can of black beans. If replaced, skip soaking & 1 ½ hour cooking.

LABELS FOR JARS - FOR PHOTOCOPYING

BLACK BEANS & RICE

Add Ons: 1 can diced tomatoes
15 c. water divided

Directions: Remove oxygen absorber.
Quart: Soak beans & soda in 4 c. water overnight. Rinse. Simmer beans in 6 c of water covered for 1 1/2 hours on low heat. (This can be done in advance) Drain. Return beans to pot, add diced tomatoes undrained, and 2 c. water. Bring to a boil. Turn heat off. Add the rest of the contents of the Quart. Let sit 5 minutes covered. Return to boil and simmer on low heat for 15 minutes.
Pint Rice: Empty the pint into a second pot and add 3 c. water. Cover and simmer on medium heat for 15 minutes. Adjust heat to low for another 15 minutes.
Assembly: Serve beans over a bed of rice.

BLACK BEANS & RICE

Add Ons: 1 can diced tomatoes
15 c. water divided

Directions: Remove oxygen absorber.
Quart: Soak beans & soda in 4 c. water overnight. Rinse. Simmer beans in 6 c of water covered for 1 1/2 hours on low heat. (This can be done in advance) Drain. Return beans to pot, add diced tomatoes undrained, and 2 c. water. Bring to a boil. Turn heat off. Add the rest of the contents of the Quart. Let sit 5 minutes covered. Return to boil and simmer on low heat for 15 minutes.
Pint Rice: Empty the pint into a second pot and add 3 c. water. Cover and simmer on medium heat for 15 minutes. Adjust heat to low for another 15 minutes.
Assembly: Serve beans over a bed of rice.

POTATO SOUP ⏱

This is a 2 Quart dinner

Quart 1
2 c. instant potato flakes

--- In baggie in jar ---
1 3/4 c. powdered milk

Add-On: 10 c. water divided

Quart 2
1 c. dried potato dices
1 c. dried sweet corn
1/2 c. parmesan cheese
2 t onion flakes
1 t parsley flakes
2 T beef bouillon
1/2 t garlic powder
1/4 t black pepper
1/4 t thyme

Directions: Bring 7 cups water just to a boil. While that is heating up, whisk 3 cups water with the powdered milk in the baggie. Once the 7 cups of water just reaches a boil, turn off heat & add contents of both jars. Stir & cover and let sit 5 minutes. Add the whisked milk, heat for about 5 to 10 minutes until well blended. Top individual bowls with shredded cheese & sour cream.

LABELS FOR JARS - FOR PHOTOCOPYING

POTATO SOUP ⏰
QUART 1 OF 2

Add-On: 10 c. water divided

Directions: Bring 7 cups water just to a boil. While that is heating up, whisk 3 cups water with the powdered milk in the baggie. Once the 7 cups of water just reaches a boil, turn off heat & add contents of both jars. Stir & cover and let sit 5 minutes. Add the whisked milk, heat for about 5 to 10 minutes until well blended. Top individual bowls with shredded cheese & sour cream.

POTATO SOUP ⏰
QUART 2 OF 2

Directions: Bring 7 cups water just to a boil. While that is heating up, whisk 3 cups water with the powdered milk in the baggie. Once the 7 cups of water just reaches a boil, turn off heat & add contents of both jars. Stir & cover and let sit 5 minutes. Add the whisked milk, heat for about 5 to 10 minutes until well blended. Top individual bowls with shredded cheese & sour cream.

POTATO SOUP ⏰
QUART 1 OF 2

Add-On: 10 c. water divided

Directions: Bring 7 cups water just to a boil. While that is heating up, whisk 3 cups water with the powdered milk in the baggie. Once the 7 cups of water just reaches a boil, turn off heat & add contents of both jars. Stir & cover and let sit 5 minutes. Add the whisked milk, heat for about 5 to 10 minutes until well blended. Top individual bowls with shredded cheese & sour cream.

POTATO SOUP ⏰
QUART 2 OF 2

Directions: Bring 7 cups water just to a boil. While that is heating up, whisk 3 cups water with the powdered milk in the baggie. Once the 7 cups of water just reaches a boil, turn off heat & add contents of both jars. Stir & cover and let sit 5 minutes. Add the whisked milk, heat for about 5 to 10 minutes until well blended. Top individual bowls with shredded cheese & sour cream.

BISCUITS & SAUSAGE GRAVY

This is a 2 Quart dinner

Quart 1

2 c. + 2 T flour
5 T dehydrated shortening
3 T powdered milk
2 T egg powder
1 scant T baking powder
1 t salt
1/2 t cream of tartar
1/4 t baking soda

In separate baggie in <u>Quart 2</u>

2 1/2 t butter powder
1/4 c. + 2 T cheddar cheese powder
1/4 c. + 2 T cornstarch
1 t milk powder

Quart 2

1 c. sausage TVP
1 c. dried mushroom pieces
3 t beef bouillon
3 T dried chopped onion pieces
1 1/2 t dried minced garlic
1 bay leaf
1/2 t Italian seasoning
1/2 t basil
1/4 t thyme (optional)
1/4 t oregano leaves
1/8 t cumin
Dash black pepper
Dash rosemary

Directions: First remove any oxygen absorber in jars.

Quart 1 Biscuits: Mix flour mixture with 1 cup water. Stir vigorously until well blended. Drop by about 1/4 cup amounts onto a greased baking sheet. You should get about 12 biscuits. Bake at 400 for 10 to 12 minutes.

Quart 2 Gravy: Whisk contents of seasoning packet into 4 cups cold water. Bring water just to a boil. Turn heat off. Empty contents of jar into hot water, cover & let sit 5 minutes. Return to a low simmer for a few minutes until tender and thickened. Remove bay leaf.

Assembly: Cut biscuits in half and top with sausage gravy.

LABELS FOR JARS - FOR PHOTOCOPYING

BISCUITS & SAUSAGE GRAVY QUART 1 OF 2 - BISCUITS

Directions: First remove any oxygen absorber in jars.

Quart 1 Biscuits: Mix flour mixture with 1 cup water. Stir vigorously until well blended. Drop by about 1/4 cup amounts onto a greased baking sheet. You should get about 12 biscuits. Bake at 400 for 10 to 12 minutes.

BISCUITS & SAUSAGE GRAVY QUART 2 OF 2 - GRAVY

Directions: First remove any oxygen absorber in jars.

Quart 2 Gravy: Whisk contents of seasoning packet into 4 cups cold water. Bring water just to a boil. Turn heat off. Empty contents of jar into hot water, cover & let sit 5 minutes. Return to a low simmer for a few minutes until tender and thickened. Remove bay leaf.

Assembly: Cut biscuits in half and top with sausage gravy.

BISCUITS & SAUSAGE GRAVY QUART 1 OF 2 - BISCUITS

Directions: First remove any oxygen absorber in jars.

Quart 1 Biscuits: Mix flour mixture with 1 cup water. Stir vigorously until well blended. Drop by about 1/4 cup amounts onto a greased baking sheet. You should get about 12 biscuits. Bake at 400 for 10 to 12 minutes.

BISCUITS & SAUSAGE GRAVY QUART 2 OF 2 - GRAVY

Directions: First remove any oxygen absorber in jars.

Quart 2 Gravy: Whisk contents of seasoning packet into 4 cups cold water. Bring water just to a boil. Turn heat off. Empty contents of jar into hot water, cover & let sit 5 minutes. Return to a low simmer for a few minutes until tender and thickened. Remove bay leaf.

Assembly: Cut biscuits in half and top with sausage gravy.

APPENDIX A – ALPHABETICAL LIST OF RECIPES

APPENDIX B – ALPHABETICAL LIST OF INGREDIENTS & ADD ONS

Ingredient	Amount for 30/60/90 day supply				Page
	30 day	60 day	90 day		
Baking Powder	7	14	21	tsp	51, 55, 65
Baking soda	1.5	3	4.5	tsp	9, 39, 45, 55, 61, 65
Barley	6	12	18	Tbs	35
Basil	6.13	12.25	18.38	tsp	11, 13, 19, 23, 27, 31, 43, 65
Bay leaf	5	10	15		21, 31, 35, 65
Beef (Ground 1 pint)	12	24	36	pints	9, 13, 17, 19, 27, 31, 33, 35, 43 x 2, 45, 59
Beef bouillon granules	53	106	159	tsp	13, 19, 27, 29, 31, 33, 35, 37, 39, 43, 49, 61, 63, 65
Beef TVP	1.25	2.5	3.75	Cups	11, 23
Bell peppers (dried & chopped)	1.58	3.17	4.75	Cups	9, 15, 29, 31, 37, 45, 59
Black beans	0.67	1.33	2	Cups	61
Black pepper	4.63	9.25	13.88	tsp	9, 11, 13, 19, 21, 23, 27, 29, 31, 33, 35, 41, 45, 47, 51, 53, 55, 57, 63, 65
Broccoli (dried)	2	4	6	Cups	23, 55
Brown / beef gravy mix	0.75	1.5	2.25	Cups	17, 33
Butter	5	10	15	Tbs	15, 41
Butter powder	11.5	23	34.5	tsp	33, 35, 65
Buttermilk powder	2	4	6	tsp	33
Carrots (dried & chopped)	3.25	6.5	9.75	Cups	21, 31, 33, 39, 43, 47, 51
Cayenne pepper	1.13	2.25	3.38	tsp	9, 11, 29, 41, 45, 47, 51, 55

Ingredient	Amount for 30/60/90 day supply				Page
	30 day	60 day	90 day		
Celery flakes	12	24	36	Tbs	21, 29, 31, 33, 35, 37
Cheddar cheese powder	1.34	2.69	4.03	Cups	23, 29, 41, 47, 51, 55, 57, 65
Chicken (1 pint)	10	20	30	pints	7, 15, 21, 29, 35, 41, 47, 49, 51, 53, 55
Chicken bouillon granules	45	90	135	tsp	7, 13, 15, 19, 21, 25, 27, 29, 41, 47, 53, 61
Chicken gravy powder	3.31	6.63	9.94	Cups	29, 41, 47, 51, 55
Chiles (4 oz can diced green)	2	4	6	Cans	53, 59
Chili powder	0.74	1.49	2.23	Cups	9, 15, 17, 27, 43, 45
Cilantro (dried)	3	6	9	tsp	25, 43
Cinnamon	0.0625	0.125	0.1875	tsp	37
Corn (15 ounce can)	1	2	3	Cans	17
Corn (sweet corn dried)	5.17	10.33	15.5	Cups	31, 33, 37, 43, 45, 51, 61, 63
Cornstarch	2.02	4.04	6.06	Cups	9, 11, 13, 19, 23, 27, 49, 57, 65
Cream of tartar	1	2	3	tsp	55, 65
Cumin	6.13	12.25	18.38	tsp	17, 25, 37, 45, 49, 65
Egg powder	5.5	11	16.5	Tbs	11, 55, 65
Flour (all purpose white)	20.63	41.25	61.88	Cups	23, 49, 51, 53, 55, 57, 59, 65

Ingredient	Amount for 30/60/90 day supply				Page
	30 day	60 day	90 day		
Garlic powder	0.41	0.82	1.23	Cups	7, 11, 13, 15, 17, 19, 21, 23, 25, 27, 29, 31, 33, 35, 37, 39, 41, 43, 45, 47, 49, 51, 53, 55, 57, 59, 63
Garlic (dried minced)	2.5	5	7.5	Tbs	9, 37, 65
Garlic salt	2.38	4.75	7.13	tsp	17, 29, 41, 47, 51
Gluten flour	6	12	18	Tbs	11
Great northern beans	2.5	5	7.5	Cups	39, 45
Green Beans (14 oz can)	2	4	6	Cans	15
Green beans (dried)	1	2	3	Cups	31, 33
Italian seasoning	29	58	87	tsp	7, 9, 11, 15, 21, 23, 29, 41, 47, 51, 55, 57, 65
Ketchup	0.5	1	1.5	Cups	43
Lemonade powder with sugar	5	10	15	tsp	25, 39
Lentils	1.13	2.25	3.38	Cups	7, 35
Macaroni	18.46	36.92	55.38	Cups	7, 13, 17, 19, 21, 27, 29, 35, 47
Marjoram	0.5	1	1.5	tsp	33
Milk (non-instant dry)	6.90	13.79	20.69	Cups	13, 19, 27, 29, 41, 47, 51, 55, 63, 65
Mushrooms (dried)	4.88	9.75	14.63	Cups	7, 11, 13, 21, 31, 55, 65
Olive Oil	1.25	2.5	3.75	Cups	11, 23, 49, 53, 57, 59
Olives (small can; sliced)	3	6	9	Cans	49, 57, 59

Ingredient	Amount for 30/60/90 day supply				Page
	30 day	60 day	90 day		
Onion (dried & chopped)	4.05	8.10	12.16	Cups	7, 9, 11 13, 15, 17, 19, 21, 25, 27, 29, 31, 33, 35, 37, 43, 45, 47, 51, 53, 55, 59, 61, 63, 65
Onion powder	0.5	1	1.5	tsp	45, 55
Oregano	0.32	0.64	0.96	Cups	7, 9, 11, 15, 17, 23, 29, 33, 41, 43, 45, 47, 49, 51, 57, 65
Paprika	2.5	5	7.5	tsp	11, 15, 23, 45, 57
Parsley	0.35	0.70	1.06	Cups	
Parmesan Cheese	2.38	4.75	7.13	Cups	7, 11, 19, 23, 57, 63
Parsley	5.50	11	16.5	Tbs	7, 13, 15, 19, 23, 27, 35, 63
Peas (dried)	1.5	3	4.5	Cups	31, 33, 51
Pepperoni TVP	0.5	1	1.5	Cups	23
Pinto beans	0.5	1	1.5	Cups	45
Potato dices (dried)	2.25	4.5	6.75	Cups	39, 51, 63
Potato flakes (instant)	4.5	9	13.5	Cups	33, 63
Ranch dressing mix	4	8	12	Tbs	45
Red or kidney beans	3	6	9	Cups	9
Refried bean flakes (dried)	5.5	11	16.5	Cups	37, 59, 61
Rice (long grain white)	12.04	24.08	36.13	Cups	15, 21, 25, 29, 31, 35, 37, 41, 43, 47, 61
Rosemary	0.56	1.13	1.69	tsp	39, 65
Salt	0.33	0.66	0.98	Cups	9, 11, 23, 25, 31, 33, 49, 51, 53, 55, 57, 59, 65
Sausage TVP	2.25	4.5	6.75	Cups	11, 23, 65

Ingredient	Amount for 30/60/90 day supply				Page
	30 Day	60 day	90 day		
Seasoned bread crumbs	5.5	11	16.5	Tbs	11, 23
Seasoning salt	1	2	3	tsp	45
Shortening powder	18	36	54	Tbs	51, 55, 65
Sour cream powder	1.09	2.19	3.28	Cups	13, 29, 41, 47, 51, 53, 55
Spaghetti (1 pound package)	1	2	3	packages	11
Split peas	6	12	18	Tbs	35
Sugar (white)	2.5	5	7.5	tsp	11, 51
Taco seasoning	6	12	18	Tbs	59, 61
Taco TVP	0.25	0.5	0.75	Cups	59
Thyme	3.79	7.58	11.38	tsp	13, 15, 19, 27, 31, 35, 39, 63, 65
Tomato powder	2.38	4.75	7.13	Cups	9, 11, 19, 23, 33, 35, 57
Tomatoes (14 oz can diced)	19	38	57		9 x 2, 11, 17 x 2, 25, 27 x 3, 31, 43 x 2, 45, 49, 53, 57, 59, 61
Tomatoes (28 oz can crushed)	1	2	3	Cans	37
Tomato Sauce (15 oz can)	1	2	3	Cans	49
Tortilla chips	2	4	6	Bags	17, 25
Vegetables (15 oz can; mixed)	1	2	3	Cans	13
Yeast (4 oz jar)	1	1	1	Jar	23, 57

Note: The 30 day supply amounts listed in Appendix B are assuming you are doing each recipe once. The 60 day supply amounts are assuming you are doing each recipe twice. The 90 day supply amounts are assuming you are doing each recipe three times.

DINNER IS IN THE JAR

Visit us on the internet at:
www.DinnerIsInTheJar.com and *www.FoodStorageRecipes.org*

If you enjoyed *Dinner Is In The Jar*, you may also enjoy Mix-A-Meal.   The Mix-A-Meal Cookbook shows you how to make a variety of delicious mixes. It also shows you how you can convert your own recipes into mix recipes. Mix-A-Meal can be purchased at www.FoodStorageRecipes.org.

You may also enjoy, *Bread In A Bag*. Learn how to create artisan rounds, flavorful wheat loaves, tender buttery brioche, crescent rolls, chewy bagels, English muffins, and more, all with ingredients safely sealed in bags, ready to make at any time!

Bread In A Bag: Book Two is a companion book to "Bread in a Bag". Store ingredients for great sourdough breads, muffins, wheat-free breads, crackers, quick-breads and much more!

2080894R00040

Made in the USA
San Bernardino, CA
08 March 2013